THE JACKSON GENERALS

THE JACKSON GENERALS

Minor League Baseball in Jackson, Tennessee

Kevin D. McCann

Copyright © 2012 Kevin D. McCann
All rights reserved
Published by BrayBree Publishing Company LLC
P.O. Box 1587
Dickson, Tennessee 37056-1587
Visit our website at www.braybreepublishing.com

No part of this book may be reproduced, stored in or introduced into a retrieval system or transmitted in any form by any means (electronic, mechanical, photocopying, recording, or otherwise) without the prior written permission of the copyright owner.

ISBN-13: 978-0-9671251-7-6
First edition 2012
Printed in the State of Tennessee and the United States of America

Photograph Credits

Author's Collection, Jim Bailey, Fred Baker, Albert Merkel, Walt Mestan, Cam Mullen-Oates, Michael Perryman, Bernice Webb Thompson, and Library of Congress Prints and Photographs Division. Jackson Generals player photos and team logos (including the West Tenn Diamond Jaxx) courtesy of the Jackson Generals.

This book is dedicated to the memory of a true Jackson Generals fan, a wonderful gentleman, and a good friend.

James Vernon Bailey
1938-2012

Contents

	Preface	ix
1	The 1935 Season	1
2	The 1936 Season	7
3	The 1937 Season	15
4	The 1938 Season	22
5	The 1939 Season	27
6	The 1940 Season	34
7	The 1941 Season	43
8	The 1942 Season	50
9	The 1950 Season	55
10	The 1951 Season	65
11	The 1952 Season	72
12	The 1953 Season	78
13	The 1954 Season	85
14	Baseball is Back	92
	Generals by the Numbers	99
	Bibliography	109
	Index	111

Preface

Thirteen years ago, my first book on professional baseball in my hometown of Jackson, Tennessee, *Jackson Diamonds*, was published. At the time, the West Tenn Diamond Jaxx was beginning its second season after the Double-A franchise once known as the Memphis Chicks had come to town. A lot has changed since: the Jaxx hosted the Southern League All-Star Game in 1999 and a year later won the league championship. Pitching phenom Mark Prior and Cubs slugger Sammy Sosa came to town. Team ownership changed hands three times. The Seattle Mariners replaced the Chicago Cubs as the team's major-league affiliate. Through it all, the Jaxx built a winning tradition with a league pennant, four division titles, six playoff appearances, and 47 future major-leaguers on its roster.

But having researched Jackson's baseball history, I always hoped one day the team would bring back the name of the Jackson Generals. So I was excited to hear that the name would indeed return for the 2011 season, and I was honored that the team would asked me to be at Pringles Park for the big announcement on September 6, 2010.

Still, it's been almost 60 years since the Generals last played at the present-day West Tennessee State Fairgrounds—when the team lost 26 straight games during the disastrous 1954 season—and only the older fans remembered them. Therefore, this book is meant for today's fans that they may know the colorful history of the original teams and the players who played at pre-World War II Lakeview Park and Municipal Park in the 1950s.

I've been blessed to meet several former players, fans, and their families, and all have graciously shared with me their memories of the Generals and photographs and memorabilia from their personal collections. Among these have been: Ernest Ankrom, Clyde Barger, Gene Bennett, Bearl Brooks, Mike Conovan, Carroll Drostie, Earl Gearhardt, Charley Graves, Ray Haynes, Dominic Italiano, Richard Janasky, Charlie Johnson, Emil Kirik, James Kluck, Lou Lukasiuk, Walt Mestan, Mike Milinazzo, James Murdaugh, Vince Pankovits, Maurice Partain, Charle Re, Robert Samaras, Joe Wesche, and Howard Whitson. Spouses and family members included: Albert Merkel, Cam Mullen-Oates, Michael Perryman, Betty Seawright, Bernice Webb Thompson, Mrs. Archie Williams, and Mrs. Porter Witt. Others who gave their time for interviews or assisted with research include: Harbert Alexander, Fred Baker, Vasco Camp, Pam Dennis, John D. Graham, Maurice Stansell, James Scott, and Jack Darrel Wood. Ronnie Peach, expert on the Owensboro Oilers Kitty League team history, took time to track down several box scores in Owensboro that helped me complete the Generals by the Numbers section. A special thanks goes to Jim V. Bailey, who was the team batboy in 1953. He loved the Generals as much as I do, and we spent many enjoyable hours talking about the Kitty League.

The Jackson Generals: Minor League Baseball in Jackson, Tennessee is adapted from my previous book, *Jackson Diamonds*, but with additional photographs and new information that wasn't available when it was first published. I hope this book will give fans of the present-day Generals a better appreciation of Jackson's minor-league baseball heritage.

1935

Finish		Record	Pct.	GB
Fourth	(1st Half)	(21-23)	.477	3.5
First*	(2nd half)	(29-19)	.604	—

*Jackson was disqualified when it was determined that the team exceeded the league limit for higher classification players on its roster.

Managers	Record	Pct.
Tony Leidl	(4-5)	.444
Joe Wesche	(15-16)	.484
Wilbur Bickham	(31-21)	.596

Attendance	Lg Rank
Not available	

Starting Lineup

C	Guy P. Jones	.260 BA, 31 RBI
1B	Jimmy Lovelady	.222 BA
2B	Carl Sikes	.315 BA, 22 SB
3B	Grover Resinger	.292 BA, 24 RBI
SS	Mutt Durdin	.216 BA
LF	John Surgaliski	.262 BA
CF	James "Bull" Liddell	.260 BA, 54 RBI
RF	Tony Leidl	.291 BA, 45 RBI

Pitching Staff

RH	Joe Wesche	(12-8)
LH	Buford Taylor	(9-8)
RH	Jesse Webb	(9-6) 127 SO
RH	Tom "Cy" Williams	(7-6)
LH	Wilbur Bickham	(6-1)

Top 10 Batters and Top 5 Pitchers

Batter	BA	G	AB	R	H	2B	3B	HR	RBI	SB
Carl Sikes	.315	78	337	62	106	15	6	3	34	22
Harold McCoy	.312	28	109	28	34	9	3	0	10	5
Grover Resinger	.292	38	137	26	40	10	2	1	24	4
Tony Leidl	.291	80	313	47	91	18	8	5	45	4
John Sugaliski	.262	43	164	22	43	5	2	2	9	5
Guy P. Jones	.260	83	289	30	75	12	4	1	31	3
Jim (Bull) Liddell	.260	80	308	45	80	10	14	4	54	7
Julian Bray	.257	33	105	11	27	1	2	1	18	5
Wilbur Bickham	.245	36	102	12	25	4	1	0	12	3
Earl W. Hahn	.237	24	93	13	22	3	3	0	11	2

Pitcher	ERA	G	IP	W	L	CG	ER	Sh	BB	SO
Wilbur Bickham	1.66	17	76	6	1	3	14	0	19	51
Aubrey Carter	2.20	6	49	5	1	5	12	0	6	26
Joe Wesche	2.87	24	172	12	8	17	55	1	39	132
Buford Taylor	3.38	26	160	9	8	11	60	1	47	114
Jesse Webb	3.74	24	142	9	6	8	59	1	51	127

Despite the hardship of the nation during the Great Depression, the minor leagues flourished, thanks in large part to the introduction of night baseball. Jackson enjoyed this prosperity when the Kitty League was revived in 1935. Prospective team owners met at the Davy Crockett Hotel in Union City, Tennessee, on April 28 and elected Dr. Frank H. Bassett to once again serve as league president. The cities of Jackson, Lexington, and Union City, Tennessee and Paducah and Hopkinsville, Kentucky were awarded franchises. Supporters at Cairo, Illinois, applied for membership but opposition from a local softball league and difficulty securing the local diamond led league officials instead to award the sixth club to the town of Portageville in southeast Missouri.

A 92-game split-season schedule was adopted, with the winners of the first and second halves meeting in a championship playoff at the end of the season. Each club could start with up to 18 players, but had to conform to the 14-player limit twenty days later. Only three "class" players (those with more than 10 games of professional experience) were allowed per team. Night games were approved but only Jackson and Union City had lighting equipment installed at their ballparks. Admission to league games was 25 cents. "I expect to have every club finish the season," Dr. Bassett told the fans, "and assure you that every effort will be made not to have a repetition of the league's failure twelve years ago."

The first professional night game in Jackson was played on May 22, 1935, when the Generals opened their inaugural season against the Lexington Yanks. Among the 2,000 fans in attendance were Southern Association president John D. Martin and Warner Brothers motion picture actress Ann Robinson, who threw out the first ball. The Yanks (renamed the Giants a few days later) beat the Generals 10-7 and went on to sweep the three-game series. Former Jackson Midwests right-hander Jesse Webb, pitching in his professional debut, tossed a three-hitter on May 26, striking out six and walking six to beat the Hopkinsville Hoppers 6-5 and give the Generals their first victory.

After managing the team for the first ten games of the season, outfielder Tony Leidl resigned and was replaced by pitcher Joe Wesche. The Memphis right-hander had already lost his first two starts and the burden of being the new skipper only added to his pitching woes. "I just couldn't pitch and try to worry about the ball club," he recalled.

Wesche's managerial debut came against the Union City Greyhounds on May 31. For the first five innings, Generals left-hander Buford Taylor and Greyhounds right-hander R.W. "Bubba" Mason pitched dual no-hitters. A scratch hit in the sixth erased Taylor's no-hit bid but Mason continued his masterful pace the rest of the game. It remained scoreless until the ninth inning when Generals shortstop Matt Durdin, trying for an inning-ending double play, threw to first base too late as the only Union City run scored. Mason's no-hitter stayed intact and the 'Hounds won, 1-0.

Generals Fact
Generals LHP Buford Taylor and Union City RHP "Bubba" Mason pitched dueling no-hitters on May 31. Taylor lost the game on an error.

The Generals spent the first month of the season only a few games under .500 but could not win consistently enough to climb up in the standings. A two-game sweep over the visiting Paducah Red Birds in mid-June elevated them into third place with a 13-12 record as the league-leading Lexington Giants came to town for two games. Young Arkansas right-hander

Hartle Gilland

The Generals were owned by Hartle G. Gilland, a Bemis entrepreneur who also owned the Lakeview Cafe and the Lakeview Tourist Camp. Both properties were across the street from Lakeview Park, where the team played their home games. Located on U.S. Highway 45 South at the site of the present-day Bemis Square Shopping Center, the ballpark was originally built for his independent team, the Jackson Midwests (named for the local Midwest Dairy Products Corporation) in 1933. Lighting equipment was installed the following spring to bring night baseball to Jackson.

Like most minor league team owners during the Depression, Gilland had to be especially creative and innovative to attract fans to the ballpark. One incentive he used was giveaways, offering everything from free baseballs to cash and once even an automobile. Longtime Generals pitcher Jesse Webb recalled how the winner was determined: "They would scatter the tickets all over the ground," he remembered. "Then a blindfolded man went out there with a stick with a nail in the end of it and gouged it down. There was your winner."

Gilland improved on the traditional Ladies' Day promotion by offering free admission to local youngsters fifteen and under on Kids' Night. When attendance was particularly low in 1939, he held Mens' Night, inviting the ladies to bring their husbands or beaus to the ballpark, and drew its largest crowd ever. He also staged several "nights" to honor individual players and invited fans to bring them gifts. Among those honored were Dutch Welch, Jesse Webb, Ellis Kinder, and Mickey O'Neil. When he wasn't on Lakeview Park's public address system talking to the fans, he was outside trying to draw more in. "Every time they played at night," Generals batboy Fred Baker recalled, "he'd be on the streets in a car with a microphone inside and speakers on top, advertising the ballgame."

Hartle's older brother, Shaler Newbern Gilland, helped him operate the Generals. "Preacher" was a versatile jack-of-all-trades for the ballclub, serving as team vice-president, secretary, groundskeeper, and holder of the game balls for the umpires. But his most important role was that of chief scout. His seniority as a switchman for the Illinois Central Railroad allowed him to travel throughout Tennessee, Arkansas, and Mississippi searching for potential talent. His best find was a curly-haired Arkansas hurler named Ellis Kinder, who went to play twelve years in the major leagues.

Cy Williams, Jackson's best pitcher in the first half, held the Giants to four hits as left fielder John Surgaliski's solo home run, the first ever by a Jackson player at Lakeview Park, helped the Generals edge out a 3-2 victory. Tony Leidl and "Bull" Liddell each homered and drove in four runs in their 10-3 route the next day, moving them only a half game out of first. But a six-game losing streak dropped them into fifth and out of the pennant race the rest of the first half. They finished in fourth place at 21-23, only 4½ games behind Lexington.

The Generals' leading power hitter during the season was center fielder James "Bull" Liddell. The 23-year-old Wylam, Alabama native tied for the team home run crown with fellow outfielder Tony Leidl, hitting three round-trippers and earning a spot on the Kitty League All-Star team. One amusing incident involving him took place at Hopkinsville. While playing in left field, "Bull" was attacked by a swarm of bees and fled his position in the middle of the game. The 6' 2" 204-pound outfielder refused to return until a search party determined that the bees were gone.

At the end of the first half, Wesche willingly relinquished the managerial reins to former semi-pro teammate Wilbur Bickham, who took over on July 5. The Franklinton, Louisiana native was an eight-year minor league veteran, at one time having played for the Memphis Chicks. Like most managers, Bickham enjoyed sparring with the umpires and was tossed from his fair share of games during his two seasons with the Generals. Once ejected, however, a player or manager was supposed to leave the ballpark. After being thrown out at Hopkinsville late in the season, he complied with the rule and walked across the street to a house beyond the outfield fence. There he positioned himself in a second-story window and guided his team unobserved by the umpire the rest of the game.

Wesche celebrated his liberation by hurling a five-hit, 6-0 shutout two days later at Paducah and winning his next five starts. With only a 3-5 record before Bickham took over, the rejuvenated Memphis right-hander went 11-8 the rest of the season and was named to the All-Star team. He handcuffed the league-leading Hopkinsville Hoppers on four hits and 10 strikeouts on July 25, winning 9-1 and catapulting the Generals from fourth into a second-place tie with Portageville. Another win over the Hoppers, coupled with the Pirates' 5-0 victory over Lexington, put both teams in a tie for first place.

A key contributor to the Generals' resurgence was leadoff hitter Carl Sikes. The 21-year-old Starksville, Mississippi native

SHORTSTOP CARL SIKES

joined the team with his brother Watts out of Mississippi State College in late June. He ended the season as the team's leading hitter, batting .314 in 54 games and earning a place on the All-Star team at second base. His rookie performance led the Memphis Chicks to purchase his contract at the end of the season.

During the last week of July and the first part of August, Jackson and Portageville exchanged the Kitty League lead almost daily as neither club could pull ahead of the other. The Pirates invaded Lakeview Park for a brief two-game showdown beginning on August 1 with sole possession of first place at stake. The Generals led 5-1 for the first four innings until the Missourians battled back in the next three frames to tie it, then scored three more in the top of the seventh to take a 9-6 lead. But the equally determined Tennesseans scored two in their half and three in the bottom of the eighth to win 11-9 and assume the league lead. Portageville came back to win the second game on Gene Nichols' three-hitter and force yet another first-place tie.

The see-saw battle continued through the first week of August. Jesse Webb's back-to-back victories over Hopkinsville once again gave the Generals sole possession of first, then a 9-4 loss the next day tied them with Portageville all over again. They finally shook them off for good with their 5-1 victory over Paducah on August 8 as the Missourians lost to Lexington. Though Portageville held within a game of Jackson the next two weeks, a disastrous nine-game losing skid August 19-28 (including two losses to Jackson) put an end to their pennant hopes.

> **Generals Fact**
>
> A boxing match erupted in the middle of a game vs. Hopkinsville between Generals catcher Julian Bray and Hoppers player-manager (and former football player) John Henry Suther.

The Generals had to fend off challenges from Union City and Hopkinsville in the last two weeks of the season to stay on top. Tempers ran high at Lakeview Park on August 18 as a boxing match (albeit a short one) broke out in the middle of the game. Hopkinsville player-manager John Henry Suther, trying to score from third in the second inning, steamrolled into Jackson catcher Julian Bray covering home plate and was ruled safe. Bray, not appreciating the rude treatment by the former University of Alabama football star, threw off his catching gear and took a swing at him. Suther dodged and countered with a right fist to the backstop's jaw that landed him in the dust and took him out of the game. Jackson's backup catcher was the only thing the Hoppers knocked out of the pennant race, however, as the Generals finished as the second-half champions with a record of 29-19.

But the championship was taken from Jackson due to a league rule violation. After their August 28 doubleheader loss to the Generals, Union City officials protested the two games, claiming that Jackson had too many class players on its roster. Similar protests were filed by Portageville and Hopkinsville. Generals vice-president "Preacher" Gilland denied the charge, claiming that the team's only class players were Manager Bickham, outfielder "Bull" Liddell, and pitcher "Bubba" Mason. Outfielders John Surgaliski and Earl Hahn were class players, he admitted, but both were on the club's suspended (or injured) list.

At a meeting of team owners and league officials, Portageville and Union City produced records from the National Association of Professional Baseball Leagues stating that Bickham, Liddell, and Surgaliski, as well as outfielder Grover Resinger and catcher Guy Jones, were all class players. Based on the evidence, league president Dr. Frank Bassett declared Jackson ineligible for the championship series with first-half pennant winners Lexington. Generals president Hartle Gilland retaliated with similar charges against every other Kitty League club. His evidence against second-place Union City (who would have been awarded the second-half pennant) resulted in its ineligibility. A similar attempt against third-place Portageville failed and the Pirates were officially declared the second-half champions.

Lexington and Portageville were scheduled to meet and decide the overall league champions, but the Giants refused to comply. Instead they arranged a seven-game postseason series with the Generals beginning in Lexington on September 5. In the first game, Joe Wesche held the Giants to seven hits while his teammates collected 13 off three Lexington hurlers to win 7-5. Both starting pitchers were pummeled for 25 total hits the next day, but Jackson emerged with an 8-5 victory. They went on to take the third game, 6-5, when a wild throw to home plate by Giants shortstop John D. Webb allowed the winning run to cross safely. The series shifted to Lakeview Park on September 10, where second baseman Carl Sikes and outfielders Tony Leidl and "Bull" Liddell each had three hits to win the fourth game, 12-11, and clinch the unofficial championship series.

1935 Kitty League Standings

First Half (May 22-July 9)

Lexington (TN) Giants	24	19	.558	—
Hopkinsville (KY) Hoppers	24	21	.533	1
Union City (TN) Greyhounds	23	21	.523	1.5
Jackson Generals	**21**	**23**	**.477**	**3.5**
Paducah (KY) Red Birds	20	24	.455	4.5
Portageville (MO) Pirates	19	23	.452	4.5

Second Half (July 10-September 2)

x-Jackson Generals	**29**	**19**	**.604**	**—**
x-Union City Greyhounds	26	22	.523	3
Portageville Pirates	25	23	.521	4.5
Hopkinsville Hoppers	22	24	.478	6
Paducah Red Birds	21	27	.438	8
Lexington Giants	19	27	.413	9

x Both Jackson and Union City were disqualified for violating the Kitty League rule against more than three higher-classification players on their roster. As a result, Portageville was awarded the second-half championship.

Split-season playoff—None was held, as first-half champion Lexington refused to play the series against Portageville.

1936

Finish		Record	Pct.	GB
Fifth	(First half)	(27-32)	.458	13.5
Third	(Second half)	(34-24)	.586	4.5

Managers	Record	Pct.
Wilbur Bickham	(23-28)	.451
Herbert (Dutch) Welch	(38-28)	.576

Attendance	Lg Rank
Not available	

Future and Former Major Leaguers
Grover Resinger
Elam Vangilder

Starting Lineup

C	Julian Bray	.302 BA
1B	Jim Murdaugh	.263 BA
2B	Carl Sikes	.314 BA
3B	Grover Resinger	.281 BA
SS	Clyde Martin	.295 BA
LF	Herbert (Dutch) Welch	.352 BA
CF	Russell Newell	.275 BA
RF	Ralph White	.283 BA

Pitching Staff

RH	Jesse Webb	(18-11)
LH	Odell (Dolly) Lambert	(7-10)
RH	Joe Wesche	(6-4)
RH	Elbert Hodge	(5-4)
RH	Wilbur Bickham	(3-2)

Top 10 Batters and Top 5 Pitchers

Batter	BA	G	AB	R	H	2B	3B	HR	RBI	SB
Dutch Welch	.352	66	267	55	94	18	3	0	35	11
Jim (Bull) Liddell*	.334	99	377	68	126	30	8	5	85	5
Carl Sikes	.314	65	283	48	89	14	4	0	35	15
Julian Bray**	.305	100	347	62	106	136	3	3	49	11
Clyde Martin***	.295	115	444	79	131	17	7	1	47	16
Ralph L. White	.283	115	474	93	134	23	11	10	94	18
Grover Resinger	.281	76	281	43	79	14	3	0	48	2
Russell Newell Jr.	.275	116	484	101	133	17	7	2	45	25
Wilbur Bickham	.263	23	57	9	15	2	2	0	10	0
James Murdaugh	.260	63	231	35	60	5	3	0	25	4

Pitcher	PCT	G	IP	W	L	CG	ER	Sh	BB	SO
Jesse Webb	.621	35	248	18	11	29	—	—	96	227
Joe Wesche	.600	13	81	6	4	8	—	—	31	64
Wilbur Bickham	.600	10	59	3	2	3	—	—	14	34
Elbert Hodge	.556	10	71	5	4	5	—	—	20	38
Odell Lambert#	.545	37	187	12	10	10	—	—	64	125

* Includes statistics with Hopkinsville Hoppers
** Includes statistics with Mayfield Clothiers
*** Includes first-half statistics with Portageville Pirates
\# Includes stats with Lexington Giants

The Kitty League added two new clubs in 1936 to make it an eight-team circuit. Originally the cities of Mayfield, Kentucky and Cape Girardeau, Missouri were chosen, but the latter could not present its required cash forfeit before the season began and was dropped. Among the new candidates for the franchise were Owensboro and Fulton, Kentucky and Corinth, Mississippi. At a meeting of team owners and league officials on April 22, the Jackson, Lexington, and Portageville ownerships favored Corinth's admission but were outvoted by Hopkinsville, Paducah, Mayfield, and Union City, who sought Fulton's inclusion. Despite losing the berth, Owensboro purchased the Portageville franchise in mid-season and transferred it there.

The league increased its schedule to 120 games but kept the split-season format and the playoff between the winners of each half. Lexington and Paducah joined Jackson and Union City as the only teams able to host night baseball. Four teams, including the Generals, established working agreements with a major or minor league organization: Union City with the St. Louis Cardinals, Paducah with the Cincinnati Reds, Mayfield with the Brooklyn Dodgers, and Portageville with the Nashville Vols of the Southern Association. Jackson signed an agreement with the Memphis Chicks, who retained the options on any players sent and could recall them at any time.

The Generals had a one-week head start on the rest of the league as they filed into camp at Lakeview Park on April 20. Construction on the new grandstand progressed as the players trained on the field. A booth was built on top for local radio station WTJS to broadcast the Generals' home games for the first time, which were sponsored by the local Coca-Cola Bottling Works. First baseman Jack Reasner arrived from Brooklyn, New York four weeks early and assisted the carpenters in its construction.

The Generals adopted a new look for their road uniforms in 1936. Rather than wear matching gray pants, the club switched to red ones with a white stripe down the side and a dark-colored cap with a red "J" above the bill. During the season, they were mocked as the "circus team" by opposing players, prompting a return to the standard gray the following season.

The Generals lost the season opener at Lexington on May 19 by the score of 11-6, despite a solo home run by outfielder Ralph White and "Bull" Liddell's 4-for-4 performance, which included two doubles, a homer, and four runs batted in. They returned to Jackson the next evening, where they beat the Giants 9-3 behind the pitching of rookie left-hander Odell Lambert.

Despite an improved offense, the team struggled throughout the first half, unable to break into the first division. Collectively they hit .280 in the first half behind the bats of "Bull" Liddell, Ralph White, Grover Resinger, rookie Russell Newell, and Julian Bray. Liddell and White

---

Don't Miss the Opening Game Tonight

Jackson Generals

vs.

Fulton, Kentucky

Game Starts 8:00 O'clock Sharp

GENERAL ADMISSION 35c
RESERVE SEATS Extra 10c
BOX SEATS Extra 25c
Special Rate On Box For 6

Fulton Will Also Play Here Tomorrow Night

Lakeview Ball Park

were a formidable one-two punch in the heart of the Generals' lineup. Liddell, described by one newspaper as Jackson's "loud speaking center fielder," hit .306 with two homers and 45 RBIs before his release on July 28. White was Jackson's first bonafide home run hitter, sending 10 circuit clouts over Kitty League fences and driving in 94 runs. In addition, the Florence, Alabama native legged out 11 triples, swiped 18 bases, and hit a respectable .283 for the year.

The problem was an ineffective pitching staff, which had been their strength the previous season. Bickham went through several unreliable hurlers searching for an effective supporting cast for starters Jesse Webb and Joe Wesche, who shouldered most of the pitching burden. Ironically, one of his spring training castoffs, left-hander Elmer Wenning, won 12 games for the Fulton Eagles. Webb tied Paducah's Allen "Shorty" Hayes for the league lead in victories with 18 and was the only hurler to break the 200-strikeout mark, fanning 227 during the season. Southpaw Buford Taylor, who tied for the team lead with 11 victories the year before, struggled with an 0-1 record before his release. Former Freed-Hardeman College player Odell Lambert searched for his control most of the time and was a lackluster 7-10 before his release in August.

JIM KELL MODELS THE INFAMOUS RED "CIRCUS" PANTS WORN BY THE GENERALS IN 1936

Veteran Joe Wesche was 6-4 during the first-half, but a practical joke early in the second half ended his professional career. "A guy snatched a chair out from under me," he remembered. "[It] snapped my elbow out is what it did. It didn't break it, but my fastball went out the window." The team placed him on the suspended list until mid-August, when he was put back on the roster but did not play the rest of the season. He made a brief comeback attempt in 1937, but after pitching in only one game (a 5-3 loss at Union City in which he struck out five, walked three, and allowed ten hits), he switched to semi-pro ball, playing several years for the Ford Motors V-8 club in Memphis. In one memorable game with the Generals, Wesche was thrown out by the home plate umpire in only the first inning. He was so frustrated with the balls-and-strikes calls he was receiving that he threw his glove at the umpire and was promptly tossed before recording the first out.

The Generals held third place for most of May and even managed to gain a three-way tie for second after their 24-5 romp against Mayfield on May 28. Having lost 18-9 to Hopkinsville the previous night, they pounded the Clothiers for 18 hits and took advantage of nine errors in the victory. But the team dropped 12 of their next 20 games to fall into sixth place, where they spent much of the first half.

One of the surprises of the season was 18-year-old Russell Newell Jr., who beat out veteran Earl Hahn for the left field position the first week of the season. The Memphis native was a third generation ballplayer, his father being a former pitcher with Shreveport of the Southern Association and his grandfather a shortstop with the old Memphis Chickasaws. He was shifted to center and inserted in the leadoff spot during the second half to take advantage of his speed, but was briefly moved to cleanup when his hitting emerged. Both traits drew the attention of scouts from the Memphis Chicks and the New Orleans Pelicans of the Southern Association. The left-hand hitting outfielder hit .275 overall with seven triples, two homers, 45 RBI, and led the team with 25 stolen bases. He would have had three homers had he touched third base against Fulton on May 22. He also had a 19-game hitting streak during the first half and stole four bases in the second game of a June 24 doubleheader against Hopkinsville.

> **Generals Fact**
> Former General "Big Jim" Murdaugh set a collegiate basketball record by scoring 78 points in a single game for Freed-Hardeman College against Bethel College on Aug. 11, 1938. The Lions won, 115-30.

Bickham shuffled his lineup constantly due to league restrictions on class players, injuries, or poor play. His infield suffered constant turnaround with four different first basemen, five different second basemen, and four different shortstops used in a two-month span. After .200-hitting Jack Reasner was released, the Jackson skipper tried 19-year-old rookie Jim Murdaugh at first base. Though he had played for the local independent club for five years, the 6' 3" Bemis native was better known as a star basketball player for Freed-Hardeman College. There he set a national collegiate record by scoring 78 points in one game (62 points in the second half alone). Jim lived within walking distance of Lakeview Park and the players often walked past his home before and after games. They played catch with him at the ballpark and even let him pitch batting practice before he joined the club.

"Big Jim" Murdaugh

After two weeks in the starting lineup, Jim was tenth in the Kitty League with a .356 average. He went 4-for-5 with four straight hits, two stolen bases, drove in a run, and scored two in the Generals' 11-5 victory over Portageville. But by the end of June, his average had dropped and Bickham moved third baseman Grover Resinger across the diamond to replace him. Overall, Jim hit .263 in 69 games with 25 RBI for the season. He was released to Lexington the next spring and moved with the team when it was transferred to Bowling Green,

Kentucky in 1939. A broken leg suffered while playing in the Alabama State League later that season ended his baseball career. But he remained active in local sports, officiating high school and college basketball games for over 50 years, and was inducted into the Freed-Hardeman University Men's Basketball Hall of Fame in 1988 and the Jackson-Madison County Sports Hall of Fame in 1989.

Unable to break the Generals from their first-half stalemate, Wilbur Bickham resigned as manager on July 8. His players were "the best bunch of boys out there that any manager ever had," he said, "and they gave everything they could in every game. It just looked like I couldn't win and I thought some other manager might be able to do better." His successor was Herbert M. "Dutch" Welch, who had piloted the Jackson Midwest independent team in 1934 and managed the Portageville Pirates to the second-half championship a year later. A native of Dyersburg, Tennessee, "Dutch" began his professional career with the Fulton Railroaders of the Kitty League in 1922 and played with the Paris Parisians the next year. He was sold to the Danville, Illinois club of the Three-I League in 1923 for $750. A Danville newspaper described him as "one of the greatest free swingers that has come up in recent years." A year later, he was sold to the Boston Red Sox for reportedly "the largest (sum) ever obtained for an infielder" in the league's history up to that time. He hit .289 with a triple and two RBIs as a September call-up in 1925, but committed eight errors at shortstop.

When Welch assumed the managerial reins, the Generals were in sixth place with a 23-28 record. He rearranged the lineup, moving young Russ Newell into the leadoff spot and rotating himself between left field and third base while "Bull" Liddell was on the suspended list with a side injury. An early indication of his aggressive style were the two double steals executed during the Generals' 20-5 route over the Fulton Eagles on July 11. Both involved Carl Sikes, who had three stolen bases in his return to Jackson. The speedy second sacker had been sent on option from the Memphis Chicks, who felt he needed more playing time. The Generals won five of their last nine games of the first half under their new skipper to finish in fifth place at 27-32, 13½ games behind first-place Union City.

The team began the second half with two losses to the Greyhounds, then won their next five games to rise above .500 for the first time all season. On July 22, left-handed pitcher Leland McDevitt held Hopkinsville to eight hits while his teammates collected 10 to beat the Hoppers 9-4 and take the league lead. The game was highlighted by an unusual "home run" by shortstop Clyde Martin. With catcher Bo "Mutt" Quillen on first base, the Jackson shortstop laid down a perfect bunt to advance him to second. Martin was called safe at first as Hoppers pitcher Walter Knickmeyer threw high to the first sacker and the ball got away. He scrambled to second, then to third as Quillen raced home. The throw went past the catcher, allowing Quillen to score, and Martin sprinted across the plate with the second run. But their hold on first place was brief as the Kentuckians came back the next day to beat Odell Lambert 7-3 and dropped Jackson back into second.

An interesting game took place at Turner Field in Union City on July 15. Leland McDevitt, starting in his first game for Jackson, walked the first three batters he faced but managed to keep them from scoring. He did the same thing in the second inning, but

Generals Fact
During a game at Union City, base hits were lost behind the Turner Field scoreboard and inside a tree!

uncorked a wild pitch that allowed the runner on third to score. The left-hander later gave up a long hit to Greyhound third baseman Bobby Richards that found its way behind the right field scoreboard. Richards sprinted around the bases and across home plate as Ralph White struggled to find the ball. Fortunately for Jackson, the umpire ruled it a ground rule double.

Another ball disappeared in the sixth when "Bull" Liddell smashed a drive to right center field that got past the Greyhound right fielder and rolled into a tree against the fence. A search party consisting of Umpire Ellis Beggs and half the Union City team failed to locate the elusive orb. Liddell, who had already crossed the plate and was sitting on the Generals' bench, was called back on the field and the hit ruled a ground rule double. The contest was made even more interesting in the seventh when Ralph White lost his temper after he was called out on strikes and tried to slug the umpire.

For the first time all season, there was stability in the Generals infield. After being optioned back to Jackson, second baseman Carl Sikes provided the team with good hitting and speed at the top of the lineup, batting .314 with 35 RBIs and 15 stolen bases in 65 games. In mid-July, they acquired shortstop Clyde Martin from the Portageville Pirates. The Dexter, Missouri native made an immediate impact, going 4-for-5 in his debut against his former team (which had since relocated to Owensboro, Kentucky), with two doubles, a homer, two RBI and three runs scored. Martin finished the season at .291 with 40 RBI and 14 stolen bases for both clubs. Much-traveled infielder Bill Justice, who played for five different Kitty League clubs during the season, forced third baseman Grover Resinger's shift to first by hitting .375 during his month-long absence. The Morristown, Tennessee native stayed at third the rest of the season, hitting .299 with two home runs and 38 RBIs.

Grover "The Fox" Resinger, out of the lineup since the last week of July with malaria, returned in late August and was shifted to first base, where he provided steady defense and finished the season batting .281 with 48 RBIs. The St. Louis, Missouri native played fourteen more seasons in the minor leagues before serving as a coach under manager Enos Slaughter with the Cardinals' Triple-A club at Houston in 1960. Although he never made it to the major leagues as a player, Resinger did as a coach with the Atlanta Braves, Chicago White Sox, California Angels, and the 1968 world champion Detroit Tigers. In addition, he was a minor league instructor for the Oakland Athletics and ended his baseball career as a scout for the New York Yankees.

On July 28, the front office was forced to release the team's best run producer, cleanup hitter Jim "Bull" Liddell. The roster already had the maximum number of class players allowed by the league and his spot was needed to add a new third baseman when Resinger went down. "Just wait until I sign with one of these other clubs and come back here," he warned, "and I will smack that baseball out of sight." Liddell was true to his word. After signing with Hopkinsville, the right-hand hitting outfielder pounded his former teammates practically every time he faced them the remainder of the season. In five games against Jackson, he batted .450 with a home run, a triple, three doubles, and 10 RBIs.

Upon the suggestion of Paducah sportswriter Sam Livingston, the Kitty League held its first annual All-Star Game, with fans from each city voting on the participants. Pitcher Jesse Webb and second baseman Carl Sikes were selected as Jackson's first representatives. The Medina right-hander finished third in the voting behind Fulton's John B. Long and Union City's John Swank among the pitchers while Sikes was fifth among the position players.

THE FIRST KITTY LEAGUE ALL-STAR TEAM INCLUDED TWO GENERALS: SECOND BASEMAN CARL SIKES (FIRST ON THE LEFT, BOTTOM ROW) AND RIGHT-HANDED PITCHER JESSE WEBB (THIRD FROM THE RIGHT, TOP ROW). ON JULY 29, 1936, THE ALL-STARS BEAT THE PADUCAH INDIANS, 8-3.

The contest, sponsored by the Paducah Sun-Democrat, was held at Hook's Park on July 29. Before an estimated 2,500 fans, the All-Stars triumphed over the first-half champion Paducah Indians, 8-3. Webb pitched the last two innings, holding the Tribe scoreless and allowing only one hit. Carl Sikes played the entire game and had an RBI double, a stolen base, and was hit by a pitch.

After their one-game All-Star break, the Generals resumed their pursuit of the league-leading Union City Greyhounds, sweeping a two-game series against them at Lakeview Park on July 31 and August 1. Two days later, Jackson rallied in the ninth inning to beat Lexington 12-11 in a game that featured 37 hits, 21 of them belonging to the Generals. That same night, Fulton held the 'Hounds 8-2 to allow Jackson to move into first place. After relinquishing the lead the next day, they won their next two (including a two-hit shutout at Paducah by Jesse Webb on August 5) to reclaim it.

The Generals held first place for almost a month, winning 18 out of 28 games. Webb won four consecutive starts, including his career-high 18th victory of the season. He also contributed an "iron man" performance by starting in the first game and relieving in the second to win both ends of a doubleheader at Union City on August 9. Veteran right-hander Lester Gray, acquired from Lexington in mid-August, won his first three games with the team to finish at 3-2 (11-8 overall).

In late August, the Generals acquired former major league pitcher Elam Vangilder, who had played eleven seasons for the St. Louis Browns and Detroit Tigers, to bolster their starting pitching. The 40-year-old right-hander made an impressive debut against Mayfield on August 31. On the mound, he held the Clothiers to six hits and struck out six. At the plate, he was a perfect 5-for-5, hitting two home runs and driving in six runs. Unfortunately, it was his brightest moment with the team as he lost his next three starts, including the last game of the season to Lexington, 3-2.

The 'Hounds held close to Jackson throughout August and thanks to Fulton left-hander

Elmer Wenning's 11-strikeout performance against the Generals on September 3 were just three percentage points behind. The next evening, Jesse Webb dominated Fulton with a two-hitter and 13 strikeouts through the first seven innings. With one out in the eighth, he walked former General Earl Hahn and struck out the next hitter, Ray Clonts, but catcher Lee Keller dropped the third strike to allow him to advance to first base. Webb and Keller had a conference on the mound and chose to intentionally walk the next batter, Lindsey Wilson, and pitch to Roy Frazier, who was hitless in the game. But Webb left his toss to Keller a little over the plate and Wilson hit it into deep center field, scoring Hahn and Clonts with the tying and winning runs for Fulton.

The heartbreaking loss gave Union City back the league lead and dropped the Generals into second. They never recovered, losing five of their last eight games of the season. Their last victory was a one-hitter by left-hander Gordon Barrett against Mayfield on September 11. He took a one-run lead into the eighth inning, but three successive walks, an infield error, and a steal of home in the eighth allowed the Clothiers to take the lead. The Generals came back to tie the score in their half and won it in the ninth when the Mayfield pitcher threw wild to third base trying to catch Russ Newell, who had overrun the bag, and allowed him to score the winning run.

The Generals finished in third place with a record of 34-24, 4½ games behind Union City. The Greyhounds captured the second-half pennant amid allegations by second-place Lexington that they had exceeded the three-class player limit during the season. The protest was denied by league president Dr. Frank H. Bassett, but the first-half champion Paducah Indians refused to play Union City in the playoff. As a result, the Kitty League was deprived of its second consecutive postseason series.

1936 Kitty League Standings

First Half (May 19-July 16)

Team	W	L	Pct	GB
Paducah Indians	41	19	.683	—
Union City Greyhounds	35	24	.593	5.5
Fulton (KY) Eagles	35	26	.574	6.5
Lexington Giants	32	30	.516	10
Jackson Generals	**27**	**32**	**.458**	**13.5**
Hopkinsville Hoppers	27	33	.450	14
Portageville Pirates	25	35	.417	16
Mayfield (KY) Clothiers	19	42	.311	22.5

Second Half (July 17-September 13)

Team	W	L	Pct	GB
Union City Greyhounds	39	20	.661	—
Lexington Giants	36	21	.632	2
Jackson Generals	**34**	**24**	**.586**	**4.5**
Paducah Indians	32	26	.552	6.5
Fulton Eagles	28	30	.483	10.5
*Owensboro (KY) Pirates	26	32	.448	10.5
Mayfield Clothiers	18	39	.316	20
Hopkinsville Hoppers	18	39	.316	20

* Portageville franchise transferred to Owensboro, July 17

1937

Finish	Record	Pct.	GB
Fifth*	(63-58)	.521	11

* Jackson lost a one-game playoff after finishing the season in a fourth-place tie with the Mayfield Clothiers.

Managers	Record	Pct.
Herbert (Dutch) Welch	(63-58)	.521

Attendance	Lg Rank
Not available	

Future and Former Major Leaguers

Grover Resinger
Orlin Collier
Elmer "Mule" Shirley

Starting Lineup

C	Archie Williams	.243 BA
1B	Grover Resinger	.280 BA
2B	Stanley Hayden	.252 BA
3B	Duke Wells	.318 BA
SS	Clyde Martin	.305 BA
LF	Herbert (Dutch) Welch	.326 BA
CF	Russell Newell	.212 BA
RF	C.C. (Cy) Miller Jr.	.332 BA

Pitching Staff

RH	Jesse Webb	18-14, 2.98 ERA
RH	Orlin Collier	15-9, 2.73 ERA
LH	Porter Witt	10-5, 3.73 ERA
	Charlie Silver	5-5, 3.77 ERA
	Johnny Owens	5-9, 4.97 ERA

Top 10 Batters and Top 5 Pitchers

Batter	BA	G	AB	R	H	2B	3B	HR	RBI	SB
C.C. (Cy) Miller Jr.	.332	115	452	77	150	20	9	0	67	19
Dutch Welch	.326	111	430	65	140	26	11	1	66	17
Duke Wells	.318	91	362	54	115	18	5	4	64	7
James Murdaugh*	.310	118	436	56	135	17	4	2	44	2
Norman Veazey**	.305	85	338	46	103	11	6	1	50	5
Clyde Martin	.305	69	269	46	82	13	5	0	32	5
Harold Adair	.286	36	123	19	35	7	1	4	16	3
Grover Resinger	.280	110	410	58	115	22	1	0	50	15
Julian Bray***	.265	73	253	50	67	13	4	0	44	4
Stanley Hayden#	.252	94	349	52	88	8	5	0	39	3

Pitcher	ERA	G	IP	W	L	CG	ER	Sh	BB	SO
Orlin Collier	2.73	28	214	15	9	21	65	—	52	177
Jesse Webb	2.98	40	260	18	14	26	86	—	85	241
William Lyter##	3.39	26	154	8	9	11	58	—	49	80
Porter Witt	3.73	25	135	10	5	8	56	—	44	77
Charlie Silver	3.77	12	93	5	5	7	39	—	50	49

* Also with Lexington   ** Also with Owensboro and Fulton   *** Also with Mayfield
\# Also with Hopkinsville   \#\# Also with Lexington

At the start of the 1937 season, the only Kitty League teams not equipped to play night baseball were Mayfield, Lexington, and Hopkinsville. Both Jackson and Lexington maintained their independent status while the rest of the league signed or renewed working agreements with major or minor league teams: Union City with the St. Louis Cardinals, Paducah with the Cincinnati Reds, Owensboro with the Cleveland Indians, Mayfield with the St. Louis Browns, Fulton with Nashville of the Southern Association, and Hopkinsville with Milwaukee of the American Association. The highlight of the Generals' spring training was beating the famous House of David barnstorming club in an exhibition game at Lakeview Park 5-2, with pitchers Jesse Webb, Porter Witt, and Harve Taylor collectively holding the bearded batsmen to only four hits.

The Generals began the season at home against their traditional Opening Day rivals, the Lexington Giants, on May 11. The Lakeview Park grandstand had undergone more preseason renovations as the clubhouse was enlarged and more lights were added to increase its power to 181,000 watts. The increased visibility did little to help the Giant hitters find home plate as Jesse Webb, despite giving up 12 hits, held them to only one run. His teammates had more trouble connecting off knuckleball hurler Cecil Hutson, but made their six hits against him count for six runs and a 6-1 victory. Even Jess made contact, knocking one of Hutson's floaters for an RBI single. The slow-footed veteran then surprising the large crowd by stealing second base!

Generals Fact
The Generals started the 1937 season with 13 consecutive wins, the longest streak in club history.

The Generals won their first 13 games, the longest winning streak in club history. Stellar pitching performances by veterans Webb and Orlin Collier, together with the hitting of rookie C.C. "Cy" Miller Jr. and shortstop Clyde Martin, led the way. Collier set a Kitty League record during the streak, pitching 27 consecutive scoreless innings in his first three starts (a record later broken by Frank Hughes, who hurled 29 scoreless innings for Hopkinsville in 1948). His best outing was a three-hit, 4-0 shutout against the Owensboro Oilers, in which he struck out 14 and fanned the side to win. Center fielder Russell Newell smashed the first circuit clout of the year at Lakeview Park, a solo shot over the center field fence.

During the streak, Cy Miller led the team in hitting, batting .429 and driving in 15 runs while Clyde Martin was second at .392 with 10 RBIs. "Our boys have been traveling at a high rate of speed," Dutch Welch said, "and we have no intention of letting up all season." A week later, Oilers right-hander Bob Helvey held the Generals to three hits at Owensboro to beat them 7-2 and end the streak. The sports editor of the Owensboro Messenger attributed their winning ways to the team's use of corked bats discovered

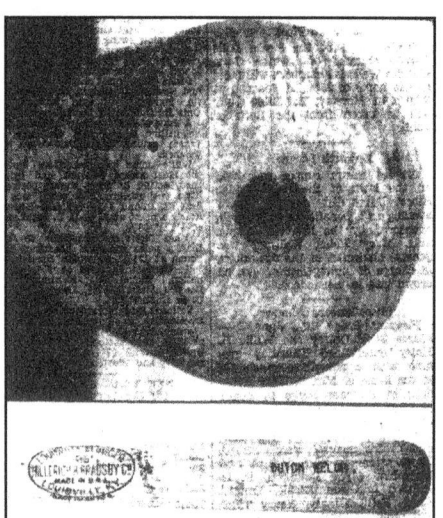

FOUL PLAY? THE CORKED BAT ALLEGEDLY USED BY GENERALS MANAGER DUTCH WELCH DURING THE TEAM'S 13-GAME WINNING STREAK.

in the visitors' dugout by curious Oilers' fans. Welch claimed that they were used in batting practice but not during games. Other teams attributed its end to the thick infield grass at Owensboro's new Miller Park, which slowed base hits down "to a snail's pace."

The loss did not stop the Generals' winning momentum. They took 25 of their next 37 games and by June 29 had built an eight-game lead over second-place Hopkinsville and a 9-½ game lead over third-place Fulton. Jesse Webb hurled a two-hitter at Union City on June 17, walking eight but striking out a career-high 19 batters to win 10-1. The Greyhounds' only run scored on Duke Wells' error as the third baseman let a ball go between his legs. After their first loss, Jackson won their next seven games, then lost two, but went on to have another seven-game win streak.

Right-hander Jesse Webb won his first nine starts of the season and finished at 18-14 for his second consecutive 18-win campaign. He led the Generals' pitching staff in victories as well as complete games (26), innings pitched (260), and strikeouts (241). He won both ends of a May 30 doubleheader with Lexington, pitching one inning's worth of relief in the first game to win 5-4, then starting the second, a seven-inning contest, for a 3-2 victory. Veteran Orlin Collier, who had a brief September stint with the Detroit Tigers in 1931, led the pitching staff with a 2.73 ERA and finished second behind Webb with 21 complete games and a 15-9 record. He broke the Kitty League single-game strikeout record on June 11 with 21 K's against the Hopkinsville Hoppers (though he lost the game 2-0), in addition to his 27 consecutive scoreless innings string. Nineteen-year-old left-hander Porter Witt of Morristown, Tennessee contributed a 10-5 record in his rookie campaign and was the team's best fielding pitcher.

The Generals' leading hitter for much of the season was right fielder C.C. Miller Jr. A Jackson native, "Cy" had been a star athlete at Lambuth College and was captain of the school's football and tennis teams. He later graduated from Vanderbilt Law School and practiced law when he was not on the diamond. The 24-year-old rookie led the club in several offensive

JESSE WEBB

Jesse Webb

JESSE THOMAS WEBB (1909-1989) was the most colorful player in Jackson baseball history, a soft-spoken, laid-back country farmer who threw a hard, rising fastball and a sweeping round-house curve. Before a game, he would often toss a few pitches in the Generals bullpen behind the home dugout (or take a nap on the grass by the grandstand, as his wife remembered), then amble toward the mound with his slow, lanky gait. He played eight seasons for the Generals and compiled a record of 125 victories against 80 losses with 1,532 strikeouts in 1,720 innings pitched. He won 17 or more games five times, including two 20-win seasons.

At a time when starting pitchers were expected to work nine innings or more, Jesse rarely finished with less than 23 complete games a season. He was durable enough to work a few innings of relief in the first game of a day-night doubleheader and then hurl a complete game in the second. "I'd pitch whenever they needed me," he remembered years later. "I stood up to it. I never did have a sore arm until my last year."

"Jesse had some zip," Generals batboy and Jackson-Madison County Sports Hall of Famer Fred Baker recalled. "He could fire that hard ball and he didn't mind throwing at you either. Then he'd sucker you in there with that curveball. You're bailing out and he's walking off the field." His rising fastball was most effective under the lights and more times than not a Jackson manager saved him for the second game of a day-night doubleheader. Once he threw an inside pitch to a batter that the umpire said hit him and promptly awarded him first base. Manager Vincent "Moon" Mullen disagreed with the call and tried to reason with the official. "It couldn't have hit him," he said. "He didn't fall down."

Jesse had the unnerving habit of getting himself into jambs, then calming getting himself out with little or no damage done. When his teammates gave him a sizeable lead, the lanky right-hander often became lackadaisical and gave up a few hits or walked a few batters to load the bases with one or no outs. Then he bore down and struck out the side. "Webb is an artist at getting himself into hot water and coming out without a scald," wrote one Jackson sportswriter.

But when Jesse had his fastball and roundhouse curve combination working just right, he could be absolutely unhittable. Although he never hurled a no-hitter as a professional, he came very close on a few occasions with two one-hitters and four two-hitters to his credit. He could also accumulate double-digit strikeout totals as shown by his 19-strikeout performance against Union City during the 1937 season.

According to former teammates, Jesse once had a chance to play for the Memphis Chicks, but squandered the opportunity. He showed up for his tryout minus a glove and spikes, so manager Doc Protho gave him money and sent him to a local sporting goods store. Instead he spent it on liquor and never returned. Hopkinsville sports editor Joe Dorris interviewed him at the end of every season and every time Jesse vowed not to play the following year. "If a man can't go up after a couple of years of Class D," he would say, "he might as well quit." Still, year after year, Jesse came back to the Generals and turned in one winning season after another.

categories, including batting average (.332), hits (150), runs batted in (67), runs scored (77), and stolen bases (19). Dutch Welch hit .326 in his first full season as skipper and paced his club in doubles (26), triples (11), and finished one behind Miller in RBIs (66).

The Generals lost their only home run hitter, Ralph White, when the disgruntled outfielder deserted the club during spring training to play semi-pro ball in Alabama. He returned to the fold in June, but was disappointing at the plate and was traded to Lexington the following season. Third baseman Duke Wells, a former football player with Arkansas A & M College, led the team with four round-trippers while driving in 64 runs (third on the team) and batting .318. His title was challenged by late-season addition Harold (Hal) Adair, who hit four of his own with 16 RBIs in the last 36 games of the season.

Injuries to key players and a sudden inability to drive in runners in scoring position helped bring the Generals down to earth. Starting catcher Archie Williams, considered one of the best backstops in the league, suffered a broken thumb trying to catch a foul tip in late June and was out for almost a month. (He returned briefly before leaving the team to work for a construction company in Commerce, Georgia) Soon after, Orlin Collier injured his right elbow trying to make a play at home plate. He returned to the starting rotation ten days later, but it took several starts before he pitched effectively again. To bolster their bench, the Generals signed second baseman Eddie Reese as an extra infielder. But the former Jackson Midwest player broke a finger just before joining the club and never played.

C.C. "Cy" Miller Jr.

Clyde Martin, the team's hard-hitting shortstop, was hit especially hard by the injury jinx. He split a finger on his right hand attempting to field a hard-hit ball, then broke the hand a few days later when it was struck by a batted ball. He returned two weeks later and received a rousing ovation from the packed Lakeview Park grandstand when his name was announced in the starting lineup and before his first at-bat. But four days later, while warming up before a game against Fulton, Martin was struck on his split finger by a fly ball and suffered a compound fracture that required six stitches. This final injury kept him on the suspended list until mid-August. Before he was forced out of the lineup, Martin had played in 216 consecutive games since the Kitty League had been reorganized in 1935.

Clyde Martin

From June 22 through July 14, the Generals dropped 18 out of 20 games. Their season-long hold on first place came to an end on July 14 with a 9-6 loss at Paducah that let Fulton move ahead of them. They kept pace with the Eagles for the next ten games, first tying them for the league lead and then beating them 5-3 in the first game of a three-game series on July 28 to reclaim it. But Fulton came back to win the next two, forcing Jackson back into second. The Union City Greyhounds swept a three-game set from the Eagles to take first for themselves, which they held the rest of the season.

In appreciation of his leadership during the season, the Generals honored their manager with "Dutch Welch Night" at Lakeview Park on July 1. The Dyersburg native received a wrist watch from Judge Frank L. Johnson as a token of appreciation in a pregame ceremony. It was the first "night" a Jackson player or manager had ever received.

Because they were in first place on July 4, the Generals hosted the second annual Kitty League All-Star Game on July 19. This year the fans were not allowed to vote on members of the squad, the selections being made instead by Owensboro manager Hugh Wise, who was chosen by the club owners as the All-Star skipper. Dutch Welch did not return from a scouting trip with team vice-president and chief scout "Preacher" Gilland in time to lead his club, so Orlin Collier took over the managerial reins for the contest. Eighteen-year-old Memphis native Clarence "Polly" Cummings took the mound for Jackson, giving up a run in the first and second innings, two in the third, and another in the fourth, then held the All-Stars hitless for the next three. He was relieved by Fred Murphy in the eighth, who allowed only one run the rest of the game.

The Generals squandered two scoring opportunities that cost them the contest. With the bases loaded in the fifth inning, shortstop Duke Wells popped up to Mayfield first baseman Eddie O'Connell, who quickly nabbed Cy Miller off the bag to end the frame. In the ninth, again with the bases loaded, Wells slapped a groundball to Union City shortstop Johnny Antonelli, who tossed the ball to second baseman George Valine to force Miller out, then threw to first base to catch Wells for the final out of the game. The All-Stars won 5-2.

Generals Fact
Players for the visiting Hopkinsville Hoppers armed themselves with bats and went after the umpire when he forfeited a game to the Generals on Aug. 24.

Jackson never regained the momentum they had at the beginning of the season and stayed in third place for much of the remainder of the season. After first baseman Grover Resinger contracted malaria for the second straight season and was forced out of the lineup for almost two weeks, they signed Elmer "Mule" Shirley to fill in. "Mule" had played two seasons with the Washington Senators and was with them during their championship season in 1924. The former major leaguer played in only four games with the Generals, batting .158 with four RBIs.

One unforgettable melee took place in the second game of a doubleheader at Lakeview Park against the second-place Hopkinsville Hoppers on August 24. Having already dropped the first game to Jackson and with the score tied 3-3 in the third inning of the second, Hoppers batter John G. Pace was hit by a Jesse Webb pitch, but the home plate umpire claimed it had hit the bat instead and ruled it a foul ball. The Hopkinsville dugout erupted and manager Paul Debnar charged the official, viciously arguing the decision. The umpire promptly tossed him from the game and ordered him off the field, but the manager refused to leave. After several more minutes of heated discussion, he declared a forfeit in the Generals' favor. Outraged, much of the Hoppers' bench grabbed their bats and charged on the field toward the umpire, who was saved only by the intervention of several Jackson players and the local police department.

The Generals finished the season in a fourth place tie with the Mayfield Clothiers, which prompted a one-game playoff to decide which would be eligible for the fourth spot in the newly adopted Shaughnessy championship series. The playoff format, created by Frank Shaughnessy of the International League to increase fan interest for clubs that were runners-up to the league champions, pitted the first-place club against the fourth-place club and the second-place team against the third-place team. The game was held at Mayfield on September 7, the day after the regular season ended. Dutch Welch gave the ball to rookie pitcher Johnny Owens, who promptly gave up four runs on two hits in the first inning without retiring a batter. Four relievers followed and eight more runs crossed the plate in the next two frames. Jackson countered with three runs in the third and one in the ninth. But with starting infielders Duke Wells and Harold McCoy having left the team after the last game, Welch was forced to use every player on his bench, including pitcher Orlin Collier in left field, and played the game under protest. The Generals lost 12-4 to finish the season in fifth place at 63-58, 11 games behind the champion Union City Greyhounds.

1937 Kitty League Standings

Team	W	L	Pct	GB
Union City Greyhounds	73	46	.613	—
Hopkinsville Hoppers	71	50	.587	3
Fulton Eagles	64	56	.533	9.5
Mayfield Clothiers	64	57	.529	10
Jackson Generals*	63	58	.521	11
Lexington Giants	60	61	.496	14
Owensboro Oilers	56	65	.463	18
Paducah Indians	31	89	.258	42.5

*Jackson lost a one-game playoff after finishing in a fourth-place tie with Mayfield

Shaughnessy playoffs—Mayfield beat Union City 3 games to none and Fulton beat Hopkinsville 3 games to 1
Finals—Mayfield beat Fulton 4 games to 1

1938

Finish	Record	Pct.	GB
Second	(74-54)	.578	1.5

Manager	Record	Pct.
Herbert (Dutch) Welch	(74-54)	.578

Attendance	Lg Rank
Not available	

Future Major Leaguers
Ellis Kinder
Ed Wright

Starting Lineup
C	Fred E. Walker	.292 BA
1B	Melvin R. (Mel) Merkel	.244 BA
2B	Vincent (Moon) Mullen	.282 BA
3B	William (Buster) Morgan	.270 BA
SS	Richard (Dick) Jones	.279 BA
LF	Herbert (Dutch) Welch	.319 BA
CF	Lou Perryman	.281 BA
RF	C.C. (Cy) Miller Jr.	.284 BA

Pitching Staff
LH	Glen Dacus	(22-8)
RH	Jesse Webb	(20-14)
RH	Lester Gray	(15-8)
RH	David Howe	(5-8)
	Richard (Dick) Stewart	(2-4)

Top 10 Batters and Top 5 Pitchers

Batter	BA	G	AB	R	H	2B	3B	HR	RBI	SB
Dutch Welch	.319	122	483	75	154	37	11	1	69	14
Fred Walker	.292	99	298	40	87	18	8	1	56	2
Archie Williams	.292	97	291	35	85	10	4	0	34	4
C.C. Miller Jr.	.284	124	493	92	140	17	8	1	57	22
Vincent J. Mullen	.282	90	291	66	82	9	10	7	57	9
Lou Perryman	.281	128	474	72	133	25	4	1	67	15
Dick Jones	.279	126	501	90	140	19	3	1	60	23
Golden Thomas	.277	54	202	28	56	8	1	1	26	3
Buster Morgan*	.270	128	470	85	127	24	6	9	85	12
Melvin Merkel	.244	99	320	46	78	18	6	5	49	2

Pitcher	ERA	G	IP	W	L	CG	ER	Sh	BB	SO
Glen Dacus	2.42	36	249	22	8	23	67	—	74	164
Lester Gray	2.91	38	226	15	8	17	73	—	62	149
Jesse Webb	3.14	37	244	20	14	22	85	—	105	225
David Howe	4.84	27	119	5	8	4	64	—	44	50
Dick Stewart	4.97	12	67	2	4	4	37	—	24	37

* Includes statistics for 65 games with the Owensboro Oilers

THE 1938 SEASON

Jackson became the only independently operated franchise in the Kitty League in 1938 when Lexington signed a working agreement with the Boston Bees of the National League. Union City switched affiliations with Paducah, taking on the Cincinnati Reds, while Paducah renewed its relationship with the St. Louis Cardinals. Hopkinsville signed an agreement with the Cleveland Indians, Mayfield with the St. Louis Browns, Owensboro with the Chicago Cubs, and Fulton with the Brooklyn Dodgers. Lexington became the only city in the league unable to play night baseball when Hopkinsville and Fulton had lighting equipment installed at their ballparks before the season began. The league owners voted to increase team rosters to 15 players and each clubs' salary limit to $1,075 a month

The Generals opened the season against Lexington at Lakeview Park on May 10. Mayor A.B. Foust threw the first pitch to catcher Lee Ware with local fan Fayette Dodd in the batter's box. Former Jackson hurler Odell "Dolly" Lambert held his ex-teammates to eight hits and beat them 4-3. But they won nine of their next 12 games and took first place from the Owensboro Oilers on May 24. Four straight losses, however, dropped them down to fourth.

A five-game winning streak was snapped on May 16 with a 6-0 loss against the Mayfield Clothiers at home. The game marked the debut of two rookies who would later lead the Generals to a playoff championship and their only Kitty League pennant. One was 18-year-old Melvin Merkel, just acquired from the Owensboro Oilers, who had 19 putouts at first base and one of Jackson's four hits in the game. The other was a right-handed pitcher from Atkins, Arkansas named Ellis Kinder, who worked three innings of relief and gave up two runs on four hits in his only appearance of the season. He had no strikeouts and no walks, but he did have a wild pitch and a balk.

> **Generals Fact**
> Future major-leaguer Ellis Kinder made his professional debut with the Generals on May 16, 1938.

Illnesses and injuries to the pitching staff during the first week of June contributed to the team's second division tumble, falling as far as seventh place by June 23. It started with promising 18-year-old rookie Ed Wright, who had an emergency appendicitis operation and missed the entire season. Jesse Webb was out several days with a painful carbuncle on his neck, then he developed a lesion on one of the fingers of his pitching hand that kept him out a few more. During a weekend series at Mayfield, right-hander Dick Stewart of Henderson, Tennessee (acquired from Lexington on May 30 for outfielder Ralph White) developed a sore arm after only an inning's work and newly acquired lefty Elmer Wenning contracted tonsillitis after only a few days with the team.

Jackson's worst defeat of the season came against Hopkinsville on June 20. Left-hander Elmer Haas, en route to a record-tying 25-win season, held them to three hits while his teammates got 18 off Webb and Stewart to hand the Tennesseans a 15-0 loss. But they fought back from a 6-1 deficit the next evening to score nine runs in the eighth inning and beat the Hoppers, 10-6.

Despite the rash of early season injuries, the Generals still had the best left-right pitching combination in the Kitty League in veteran southpaw Glen Dacus and right-hander Jesse Webb. Dacus, who reportedly won 27 games for the House of David barnstorming team two years earlier, led the circuit with his 22-8 record and 2.42 ERA. The 31-year-old Arkansas native was one behind league leader Elmer Haas in complete games (23) and led the league

The 1938 Generals. left to right (top row): Dick Jones, Lou Perryman, William "Buster" Morgan, Vincent "Moon" Mullen, Mel Merkel, Fred Walker, Archie Williams, Cy Miller. (front row): Dutch Welch, Elmer Wenning, Porter Witt, Sam Glenn, Glen Dacus, Lester Gray, Jesse Webb. The batboy's name is not known.

with 16 hit batsmen, although he did not register a wild pitch the entire season. Webb enjoyed his first 20-win season, finishing at 20-14, and his 225 strikeouts were second only to Union City right-hander Chauncey Scott's record-setting 282 K's. Right-hander Lester Gray contributed a 15-9 record as a starter/reliever with a 2.91 ERA (seventh-best in the league) and was named to the All-Star team.

The rest of the Generals pitching staff, however, combined for a 14-22 record, with none finishing at or above .500. The front office tried to correct an earlier mistake by acquiring left-hander Elmer Wenning, a 20-game winner in 1937, from Hopkinsville in May. After being cut from the Generals' spring training squad a year earlier, Wenning signed with Fulton and won 32 games over two seasons. But a bad case of tonsillitis contracted after coming to Jackson resulted in a disappointing 3-4 mark. Left-hander Porter Witt, who won 10 games for the Generals in '37, returned briefly in August after recovering from a car accident while en route to Jackson for spring training, but never regained his winning form. Right-hander David Howe led the supporting cast in victories with a 5-8 record.

Hard-hitting manager Dutch Welch led the Generals with his .319 batting average and paced the club in doubles (37) and triples (11) and tied for second in RBIs (60). Fellow outfielder Cy Miller slipped from his rookie numbers but still hit a steady .284 with 22 stolen bases and a club-leading 92 runs scored. Freshman shortstop Richard "Dick" Jones replaced Clyde Martin after he took a job back home and led the Generals with 23 steals while batting .279. Team captain Archie Williams and All-Star Fred Walker divided the catching duties, with each producing similar numbers at the plate. Both had the second-best batting averages on the club (.292) and played in almost the same number of games. But Williams, a native of Dover, Tennessee, was regarded as one of the best defensive catchers in the league with a .980 fielding percentage in 86 games. Rookie first baseman Melvin Merkel, obtained from

Owensboro early in the season, hit .244 with four home runs and 46 RBIs in 95 games.

The Generals' 21-8 record in July lifted them back into the first division. They were bolstered by the additions of second baseman Vincent "Moon" Mullen and third baseman William "Buster" Morgan, who added much-needed punch into their lineup. Mullen hit .282 in 90 games with a team-best seven home runs with 57 RBIs while "Buster" batted .270 with nine round-trippers (five with Jackson) and 85 RBIs. A three-game sweep over the seventh-place Paducah Indians and losses by Mayfield and Lexington briefly elevated the team back into the league lead on July 25. It was lost to Lexington the next day but regained four days later. Their stay at the top lasted only two weeks as the Hopkinsville Hoppers knocked them from the league pedestal on August 12.

The second-place Generals held close to Hopkinsville the last month of the season, completing a three-game sweep against them on August 24 to share the lead with Lexington, then with the Hoppers the next day. Their 14-6 victory at Mayfield two days later left them in first place alone before Hopkinsville took it back for good on August 30. Jackson stayed within striking distance, but the Hoppers' 13-game winning streak kept the Generals at bay and allowed them to clinch the pennant on September 10.

The Generals' Labor Day doubleheader on September 5 gave Jackson fans two great pitching exhibitions. The first game was played at Lexington, where young Native American right-hander Wallace Ritter held the Bees to three hits in his season debut for a 3-0 shutout. Under the lights of Lakeview Park, Jesse Webb celebrated his 29th birthday by pitching a masterful near no-hitter in the second game. His fastball and round-house curve combination enticed one ground ball after another, keeping the infielders on their toes (rookie first baseman Mel Merkel even made an unassisted double play), but he giving the outfielders the night off as only two balls came their way the entire game. Webb struck out nine, allowed only four free passes, and retired the last 13 batters he faced. A double by Bees outfielder Paul Golden forced him to settle for a one-hitter and an 8-0 shutout. Four days later, his performance was honored with "Jesse Webb Night" at Lakeview Park as fans gave the soft-spoken right-hander a variety of gifts, including groceries, clothing, and money. After the pregame ceremonies, he took the mound and beat Union City 6-1, striking out 12, walking two, and hitting a batter. The Generals finished the season two days later, 1½ games behind the league champion Hoppers with a 74-54 record.

Generals Fact
Honored before the game with "Jesse Webb Night," the Generals right-hander struck out 12 batters for a 6-1 win on September 9.

Jackson's second-place finish earned them a spot in the Shaughnessy playoffs, facing the third-place Lexington Bees in the first round. The series started on a cold afternoon at Lakeview Park on September 17. Starter Jesse Webb, who thought it was too cold to pitch, warmed up on the mound wearing a heavy, full-length overcoat until league president James Edgar "Ed" Hannephin made him take it off. Hannephin tossed the first pitch of the series to catcher Bob Bell, Jr. of the Jackson *Sun* with outspoken Generals fan Fayette Dodd in the batter's box. Rather than watch the pitch go past him, Dodd hit it on the ground and tried to beat it out for a single.

Webb and Bees knuckleballer Cecil Hutson dueled in the first game, Jess holding Lexington to three hits and striking out 11 and Huston allowing only two more with nine strikeouts.

An RBI double by third baseman "Buster" Morgan in the first inning scored Dick Jones from first for the Generals' first run. Another run added in the fourth on an error, a walk, and a single was enough to give Jackson the first game, 2-1. The Generals bombed three Lexington hurlers the next day with 15 hits, including three each by Dutch Welch and Dick Jones. Lefty Glen Dacus allowed 13 hits himself but kept them too scattered for the Bees to mount a counterattack and Jackson took the second game, 16-2. Lexington sent Cecil Hutson back to the mound to prevent their elimination from the best-of-five series, but he was pounded for 11 hits, including a solo homer by Morgan. Rookie hurler Wade Elam allowed only seven hits for a 9-0 shutout, advancing the Generals into the finals against Hopkinsville, who had already beaten the fourth-place Mayfield Clothiers.

The final series began at Hopkinsville on September 20. The Generals scored five runs in the first inning off Hoppers left-hander Elmer Haas, thanks in large part to fielding errors behind him. But Hopkinsville came back to take an 8-7 lead going into the eighth after driving Jackson starter Lester Gray and his replacement, Wallace Ritter, from the hill. The Tennesseans took advantage of more Hopper fielding miscues to push two runs across in their half of the eighth and held on to win, 9-8. The Generals had 16 hits off three Hopkinsville hurlers to win the second game, 9-5. First baseman Mel Merkel was a perfect 3-for-3 at the plate with a home run and a double, leadoff hitter Cy Miller had four hits in six at-bats, and catcher Archie Williams had two doubles in his three-for-five night. The third game was another slugfest as the Hoppers collected 17 hits while Jackson had 11 off Hoppers pitcher Johnny Schmitz, who went on to become a two-time All-Star with the Chicago Cubs and an 18-game winner in 1948. Behind 4-2, the Hoppers bunched their blows in the sixth for seven runs off reliever Lester Gray and went on to an 11-6 victory.

The series was scheduled to resume in Jackson, but the Hopkinsville management, citing the cold weather and a lack of fan interest, refused to continue. The league awarded the Generals the postseason series by forfeit but, much to the disappointment of the Jackson players, the Hoppers remained the overall league champions for the season.

1938 Kitty League Standings

Hopkinsville Hoppers	76	53	.589	—
Jackson Generals	**74**	**54**	**.578**	**1.5**
Lexington Bees	66	59	.528	8
Mayfield Clothiers	65	60	.520	9
Paducah Indians	66	63	.512	10
Owensboro Oilers	66	64	.508	10.5
Fulton Eagles	55	75	.423	21.5
Union City Greyhounds	45	85	.346	31.5

Shaughnessy playoffs—Jackson beat Lexington 3 games to none; Hopkinsville beat Mayfield 3 games to 1.

Finals—Jackson led series 2 games to 1 when Hopkinsville cancelled the series, citing cold weather and poor attendance

1939

Finish	Record	Pct.	GB
Fourth	(67-59)	.532	9.5

Manager	Record	Pct.
Vincent (Moon) Mullen	(67-59)	.532

Attendance	Lg Rank
Not available	

Future Major Leaguers
Ellis Kinder

Starting Lineup
C	Fred Walker	.251 BA
1B	Ben Drake	.264 BA
2B	Vincent (Moon) Mullen	.292 BA
3B	William (Buster) Morgan	.292 BA
SS	Richard (Dick) Jones	.313 BA
LF	James Kell	.291 BA
CF	Lou Perryman	.257 BA
RF	Paul Black	.220 BA

Pitching Staff
RH	Ellis Kinder	(17-12)
RH	Lester Gray	(16-11)
RH	Jesse Webb	(13-13)
LH	Glen Dacus	(11-10)
RH	Carl Gaiser	(4-7)

Top 10 Batters and Top 5 Pitchers

Batter	BA	G	AB	R	H	2B	3B	HR	RBI	SB
Clyde Martin	.329	40	149	18	49	6	0	0	18	1
Dick Jones	.313	109	451	65	141	19	1	1	54	42
Vincent Mullen	.292	124	435	100	127	35	5	8	92	10
Buster Morgan	.292	84	308	44	90	15	2	5	52	3
James Kell	.291	126	540	87	157	22	4	4	49	5
Ben Drake	.264	98	436	54	115	34	0	4	49	0
Lester Gray	.263	52	110	6	29	2	0	1	13	0
Lou Perryman	.257	126	486	65	125	26	7	0	43	2
Fred Walker	.251	115	426	13	107	30	2	2	64	1
Paul Black	.220	66	232	32	51	13	2	0	23	0

Pitcher	ERA	G	IP	W	L	CG	ER	Sh	BB	SO
Jesse Webb	3.09	41	256	13	13	18	88	—	94	187
Glen Dacus	3.15	28	197	11	10	15	69	—	44	136
Lester Gray	3.52	41	220	16	11	15	86	—	51	127
Ellis Kinder	3.59	30	223	17	12	13	89	—	82	200
Carl Gaiser	5.56	20	102	4	7	4	63	—	27	66

Second baseman Vincent "Moon" Mullen took over as player-manager for the Generals in 1939. The St. Louis native retained most of the infield from the previous season, with first baseman Ben Drake of Longview, Texas the only newcomer. Fred Walker, the team's top utility player the year before, took over as the starting catcher. The outfield saw two new faces, former Owensboro outfielder Jim Kell in center and Lambuth College star Will Ed Francis in right, with veteran Lou Perryman returning in left. The veteran trio of Jesse Webb, Glen Dacus, and Lester Gray, called "The Old Men's Home" by league scribes, returned after collectively winning 57 games the previous season. Rookie right-handers Ellis Kinder and Carl Gaiser and St. Louis native Bill Pavlige completed the staff.

The Generals had a successful spring training, scoring 60 runs in their last three exhibition games while holding their opponents to only two. The last was a five-inning, 23-0 massacre over the independent Humboldt Shoemakers. They began the regular season at Bowling Green, Kentucky on May 4 with left-hander Glen Dacus holding the Barons to five hits as his teammates got 10 off two Baron hurlers for a 4-2 victory. Mullen hit the first home run of the season for Jackson, a three-run shot in the third inning.

The Generals made their home debut against the Barons the next evening. More than $2,000 in improvements had been made to Lakeview Park before the season began, including a new refreshment stand at the park entrance and a new scoreboard in right center field. Ben F. Howard, the new league president, tossed the ceremonial first pitch to catcher Fred Walker behind the plate. Fan favorite Jesse Webb won the first home game of the season with a three-hit, 5-0 shutout

Jackson won their first 12 games of the season, gaining sole possession of first place with their 11-7 win at Owensboro on May 8. Mullen cautioned, however, that the teams they had beaten were not as competitive as they would be later in the season. The streak fell short of the club record 13 consecutive victories set two years earlier with a 3-2 loss at Fulton on May 19. The defeat also allowed Owensboro to take the league lead from them.

After falling into third

No. 1 Kitty League Fan

One of the most vocal hecklers at Jackson's Lakeview Park was Fayette Dodd. An Illinois Central Railroad engineer when not in the Lakeview Park stands, Dodd was a longtime baseball enthusiast and had been the president of the "Royal Rooters," a group of loyal fans who cheered for the Jackson Independents club of the 1920s. He had a loud, booming voice that carried well above the cheering and jeering of the regular spectators. "With his leather lungs, Mr. Dodd takes rooter titles in a runaway," wrote sportswriter James Goodwin, "as he bellows his harassing remarks in a low tone of voice which cannot be heard for more than two miles." Everything was fair game for his verbal outbursts, whether it was a play in the field by the opposition or details and incidents he had learned about their personal lives. Each question or remark was followed by his trademark cry: "I wanna know!" Longtime Generals fan John D. Graham remembered, "You went to the ballgame to hear Fayette as much as you did to see the game."

Fayette Dodd

Dodd enjoyed mercilessly riding umpires, opposing players, and managers alike with his scathing remarks. His favorite target was Mayfield skipper Benny Tate, whose rantings gave him a long record of fines imposed by Kitty League umpires. Whenever he took issue with one or simply showed his face outside the dugout, Fayette Dodd was ready. He loved to remind Tate about how much he already owed the league for previous outbursts and followed each remark with a villainous-sounding "Ah-Ha!" When asked about his tormentor, the former major leaguer shrugged it off. "No, he doesn't bother me. Sometimes he pops off too much, but I know he doesn't mean those things he says." He added: "For a fellow who's been heckled by Patsy O'Toole of Detroit, Dodd is nothing at all to bother about. Compared with the good ones, he's a third-rate heckler." Benny certainly must have received an earful after Dodd read those comments! Fayette Dodd had gained such notoriety that league president J.E. Hannephin proclaimed him the Number One Kitty League Fan.

place the first week of June, the team rebounded to move into second place two weeks later, just 2½ games behind the Oilers. But Owensboro, with the great pitching of bespectacled right-hander Howard Schumacher and the home run power of outfielder Eddie Urbon, proved to be resourceful in holding the league lead. Jackson kept the heat on with their 22-12 record in July (including a 10-game winning streak) to finally snatch first place from them on July 21. The team spent the rest of the month atop the standings, though leading by only 3½ games over Owensboro.

As the season progressed, rookie manager "Moon" Mullen proved to be a strict disciplinarian and did not tolerate opposition to his authority. "We have to have rules to run a ball club," he asserted, "and they must be obeyed." He confronted veterans Lester Gray and Jesse Webb during a road series at Paducah in late June for "openly breaking training rules," fined them, and sent them back to Jackson. "I don't care how good a man he is, or how much the team needs his services," Mullen said, "...his services aren't much when he don't stay in shape." The two pitchers eventually settled their differences with the manager and returned.

Despite the team's great start and its tenacious pursuit of the first-place Oilers, attendance was down considerably at Lakeview Park, forcing owner Hartle Gilland to become more creative with his promotions. One was a variation of the popular Ladies' Day promotion that gave the ladies a chance to treat the men to a game. The first-ever "Men's Night" was held on July 17 and drew the largest crowd ever at Lakeview Park. Some 3,414 spectators packed the grandstand and right field bleachers and overflowed into foul territory along the first base line. The Generals put on a show for the extra onlookers, collecting 13 hits against Hopkinsville for a 9-2 victory. Two nights later, the second largest attendance came for "Ellis Kinder Appreciation Night," which was held to honor the rookie right-hander for his pitching accomplishments during the season. He started the game but was taken out after seven innings, giving up five runs on 10 hits and losing 5-4.

GENERALS MANAGER VINCENT "MOON" MULLEN

The pitching staff finished the season with four starters winning in double figures. Ellis Kinder led the staff with his 17-12 record and tied for second in the league with 200 strikeouts in only his first full season of professional baseball. His control was not as good as it would later become, as he led the team in runs allowed (120), earned runs allowed (89), and finished second in the league with 11 wild pitches.

Veteran Lester Gray was second behind Kinder at 16-11 with 127 strikeouts, 15 complete games, and a 3.52 ERA. Though Jesse Webb's record slipped to 13-13, he still lead the team in innings pitched (256, second in the league), complete games (18), and his 3.09 ERA was the seventh-best in the Kitty. His strikeouts dipped to 187, the first time since his rookie season he had less than 200. Season-long arm soreness contributed to lefty Glen Dacus' 11-10 mark, though he finished second on the staff with a 3.15 ERA. Right-hander Carl Gaiser, released in late May, returned in July to post a 4-7 mark with a 5.56 ERA as a starter/reliever in his rookie campaign.

But it was the less-heralded Bill Pavlige that had the pitching highlight of the season when he tossed a no-hitter at Hopkinsville on July 1. The St. Louis native had been shifted around the diamond during the first two months of the season, starting the year on the mound but also spending time in the outfield and at first base when Ben Drake went on the injured list with a sprained ankle. He had only four strikeouts and one walk in the 5-0 victory. Unfortunately, Pavlige's masterpiece occurred on a Saturday night and went almost unnoticed in the Sunday morning newspapers. The right-hander bragged about his accomplishment to family and friends, but he did not have a game account to prove it. His teammates made it worse by joking that he never even threw a no-hitter. In desperation, he wrote a letter to the sports editor of the Hopkinsville newspaper asking for a news clipping to back up his claim. "If I really did pitch one," he wrote, "please send me a copy of the paper which says so." Nine days after his feat, Pavlige left the team to take a job in St. Louis.

Generals Fact
Bill Pavlige threw the first no-hitter in Generals team history against the Hopkinsville Hoppers on July 1, 1939.

Shortstop Dick Jones led the club with his .313 average and stole a league-leading 42 bases. "Moon" Mullen was the top run producer, leading the Generals in doubles (35), home runs (8), RBIs (92), and runs scored (100). His RBI total was the most by a Jackson player since Ralph White collected 94 in 1936. He was the Generals' lone representative in the league All-Star Game, playing in a utility role. Left fielder Jim Kell played in all 126 games and led the club in at-bats (540) and hits (157), finishing with a .291 average, 22 doubles, and 49 RBIs. Big third baseman William "Buster" Morgan hit .292 with five homers and 52 RBIs before his release on July 29. Catcher Fred Walker went through a prolonged batting slump during the first half of the season due to a hand injury, but he turned it around in the second half to hit .251 and finish second on the club in doubles (30) and RBIs (64). A first-half batting slump also affected center fielder Lou Perryman's numbers, though he finished with a decent .251 average. Compared to his 1938 season, the Marion, Kentucky native's stolen base and run production fell off in '39 as he stole only two bases and drove in only 43 runs, but he did lead the team with seven triples. As a team, the Generals finished seventh in the league with a .262 batting average. They were the least powerful club, finishing last in most offensive categories, but they did lead the circuit in sacrifice hits (117) for the third consecutive season.

The Kitty League pennant race grew tighter in August as Mayfield and Bowling Green joined the fray. Losing four out of seven road games in the first week and a 3-0 loss at home to Mayfield allowed the Owensboro Oilers to overtake the Generals on August 7. In that game, starter Jesse Webb had a three-hit shutout through seven innings and led 1-0. He loaded the bases on two walks and a hit in the eighth. With one out, the next batter hit a ground ball to shortstop Dick Jones that had double play written all over it. He fielded the ball cleanly but instead of throwing home to start the twin killing, he held it—apparently thinking the second baseman would be covering the bag, which he wasn't because he thought Jones would be throwing home—as the tying run scored and the runners advanced to second and third, then threw to first for the second out. Webb slammed his glove to the ground in disgust as his shutout disappeared along with the league lead. Jackson held close to gain a tie on August 15 with Mayfield just a half-game behind and Bowling Green two games out. But a heartbreaking 4-3 extra-inning loss at Fulton dropped Jackson back into second and two days later they plummeted into fourth place after a doubleheader loss to Hopkinsville.

The team collapsed in mid August, losing 17 of their last 21 games of the season. Even when Jesse Webb held Mayfield to two hits on August 26, his teammates could manage only four themselves. It took a double steal in the second inning for the Browns to score their only run of the game, but it was enough to win.

The disappointment and frustration of the Jackson fans fell squarely on Mullen and his decisions were scrutinized by them and the press. He allowed rookie Carl Gaiser to stay in a game despite having hurt his pitching arm. "Let it be known that Gaiser came out because his arm was wrenched," sportswriter James Goodwin wrote, "and not because he was, in the opinion of Moon Mullen, being hit too hard." In another game, he took Glen Dacus out in the twelfth inning, but only after two opposing runners had got on base with no outs. One fan shouted for the skipper to leave the battered southpaw in: "That's why Jackson's in fourth place!" The Generals finished the 1939 season a disappointing 9½ games behind the champion Mayfield Browns with a record of 67-59. But their fourth-place finish still entitled them to a spot in the Shaughnessy playoffs, facing the Browns in the first round.

Generals Fact
Vincent "Moon" Mullen scored 100 runs and drove in 92 runs for the Generals in 1939.

The best-of-five series began at Mayfield on September 5 with left-hander Glen Dacus on the mound for Jackson. Despite giving up four runs in the first three frames, the veteran spitball hurler settled down to hold the Brownies scoreless the rest of the game. With the score tied 3-3 in the sixth, Dacus took matters into his own hands, hitting a two-run single over first base to drive in Ben Drake and Lou Perryman and win his own game 5-3. Generals right fielder Charles Turlington misjudged a fly ball with two outs in the first inning of the second game, which proved costly as the Browns' five-run outburst resulted in a 6-4 loss. Ellis Kinder gave up two costly home runs in an otherwise good pitching performance, but still lost the third game 4-2.

The series moved to Lakeview Park on September 9, where the Generals dropped their third straight and were only one away from elimination. "Moon" Mullen's 4-for-5 performance with two doubles and two RBIs highlighted Jackson's 13-hit attack, but the Browns got the same number off the Generals' four best hurlers. Mayfield's seven-run onslaught in the fourth inning off Dacus, Kinder, and Jesse Webb put an end to Jackson's postseason championship hopes as they dropped the final game 10-5. Mayfield went on to face Bowling Green in the finals, but lost to the Barons four games to two.

1939 Kitty League Standings

Mayfield Browns	76	49	.595	—
Owensboro Oilers	75	51	.595	1.5
Bowling Green Barons*	75	51	.595	1.5
Jackson Generals	**67**	**59**	**.532**	**9.5**
Hopkinsville Hoppers	57	68	.456	19
Paducah Indians	57	69	.452	19.5
Fulton Eagles	52	74	.413	24.5
Union City Greyhounds	44	82	.349	32.5

*Lexington, TN franchise transferred to Bowling Green, KY before the season began.

Shaughnessy playoffs—Jackson beat Mayfield 3 games to 2; Bowling Green beat Owensboro 3 games to none

Finals—Bowling Green beat Mayfield 4 games to 2

1940

Starting Lineup

C	Mickey O'Neil	.291 BA
1B	Newt (Gashouse) Parker	.291 BA
2B	Earl (Country) Griffith	.224 BA
3B	Bud White	.256 BA
SS	Richard (Dick) Jones	.338 BA
LF	Al Cuozzo	.307 BA
CF	Joe Polcha	.292 BA
RF	Melvin (Mel) Merkel	.346 BA

Pitching Staff

RH	Ellis Kinder	(21-9)
RH	Jesse Webb	(17-14)
RH	Carl Gaiser	(16-11)
LH	Charley Graves	(6-4)
	Edgar Ross	(3-3)

Finish		Record	Pct.	GB
First	(First half)	(38-25)	.603	—
Fifth	(Second half)	(29-32)	.473	11.5

Manager	Record	Pct.
George (Mickey) O'Neil	(67-57)	.540

Attendance	Lg Rank
Not available	

Future and Former Major Leaguers
Ellis Kinder
Mickey O'Neil

Top 10 Batters and Top 5 Pitchers

Batter	BA	G	AB	R	H	2B	3B	HR	RBI	SB
Melvin (Mel) Merkel	.346	74	283	53	98	19	7	14	52	10
Dick Jones	.338	113	462	96	156	35	0	2	36	51
Al Cuozzo	.307	115	473	82	145	32	12	11	71	6
Joe Polcha	.292	123	446	103	130	29	8	27	97	36
Gashouse Parker	.291	118	460	74	134	23	5	27	109	2
Mickey O'Neil	.291	103	340	39	99	15	1	1	35	10
Paul Dixon	.263	47	190	30	50	6	3	2	28	10
Bud White	.256	63	238	23	61	11	1	0	29	2
Ernest Ankrom	.254	100	347	44	88	17	4	6	45	11
Earl Griffith	.224	100	353	41	79	11	2	0	25	11

Pitcher	ERA	G	IP	W	L	CG	ER	Sh	BB	SO
Ellis Kinder	2.38	32	276	21	9	29	73	—	81	307
Jesse Webb	3.82	35	254	17	14	25	108	—	113	228
Carl Gaiser	4.72	33	242	16	11	24	127	—	77	169
Edgar Ross	6.00	13	63	3	3	1	42	—	30	33
Charley Graves	9.26	20	68	6	4	2	70	—	77	68

THE 1940 SEASON

With the arrival of a new decade, the Generals were in a rebuilding mode, both off and on the field. The Lakeview Park grandstand, which had been worked on and patched up in some form or fashion almost every spring, was completely torn down and replaced with a new structure splashed with a coat of green paint. The press box was rebuilt and the tattered advertising signs on the outfield fences were mended. More lights were added to increase the park's visibility to 145,000 watts. The players sported new white flannel home uniforms with light blue pinstripes and a large blue "J." The Gilland brothers also felt a change in team leadership was needed and released "Moon" Mullen in favor of another St. Louis native, George Michael "Mickey" O'Neil.

O'Neil played nine seasons with the Boston Braves, Brooklyn Robins, Washington Senators, and New York Giants. He began his professional career in the Giants' organization, but was traded with three other players and $55,000 to Boston for pitcher Art Nehf in 1919. His best offensive season was a year later when he hit .283 in 112 games. During that season, he participated in the longest game in major league history. The May 1, 1920 contest between the Brooklyn Robins and the Boston Braves ended in a 1-1 tie after 26 innings due to impending darkness. O'Neil caught the first nine innings for Boston and was hitless in two at-bats. He spent his last major league season, 1927, under two future Hall of Fame managers: John McGraw with the Giants and Casey Stengel with the Toledo Mud Hens. Recovering from a sore arm the previous season, O'Neil tried to make it with the St. Louis Cardinals in spring training in 1930 but was released and became a coach with the Cleveland Indians.

George "Mickey" O'Neil

O'Neil's forte was working with and developing young players and relying on their speed, defense, and enthusiasm to win games. And he expected them to hustle. "You can look good losing," he once said. "But if a ball player hustles he will not lose many games. In fact, the club will have more wins than losses." Soft-spoken off the field, he was hard-nosed on it and his Irish temper flared when his orders were not followed. "He was a hard, driving type of person," Fred Baker remembered, "but he was fair." After a home run by Newt "Gashouse" Parker, Mickey gave him the big first sacker a fierce tongue-lashing when he reached home plate. The reason? Parker had connected on a 3-0 pitch.

Generals Fact
As a catcher for the Boston Braves, Mickey O'Neil caught the first nine innings of the longest game (by innings) in major-league history on May 1, 1920. The Braves and Brooklyn Robins played to a 1-1 tie in 26 innings.

"I am not going to promise Jackson a pennant winner," O'Neil said before the season began, "but I am going to promise a winning team...I'll guarantee that they will play a brand

Ellis Kinder

Ellis Raymond Kinder (1914-1968) was pitching for a semi-pro club in Scottsville, Arkansas, in 1938 when Generals vice president and chief scout "Preacher" Gilland offered him a professional contract for $75 a month. Gilland also shed three years from Kinder's age, as he felt 24 years old was "too old for a rookie."

After three seasons with the Generals and two with the Memphis Chicks, Kinder pitched in the major leagues from 1946 to 1957 with the St. Louis Browns, Boston Red Sox, St. Louis Cardinals, and Chicago White Sox.

The former Generals ace was a 23-game winner for the Red Sox in 1949, leading the American League with six shutouts and finishing fifth in the Most Valuable Player voting. He started the season with a 4-4 record and went 19-1 the rest of the way to help his new team finish in a first-place tie with the New York Yankees on the last day of the season. Boston manager Joe McCarthy gave him the start in the crucial tie-breaking game at Yankee Stadium on October 2. "You get me three runs tomorrow," he told teammate Billy Goodman, "and you've got yourselves a pennant."

Kinder held up his end of the bargain, limiting the mighty Yankees to a single run, but the Red Sox offense was shut down by New York right-hander Vic Raschi. With the pitcher's spot due up in the top of the eighth ininng, McCarthy opted for a pinch-hitter.

With him out of the game, the Yankees scored four runs off his replacement, Mel Parnell, and lost the game—and the pennant. Kinder never forgave McCarthy for taking him out. "I've played that game over and over again in my sleep," he later said. "A game like that stays with you for life."

The city of Jackson honored him with "Ellis Kinder Day" when he returned home on October 17. Local fans gave him numerous gifts and Mayor George Smith awarded him with the key to the city. Kinder brought with him a squad of major-league players to play a local independent team sponsored by the Brashers Clothing Store and managed by R.E. "Tobe" Bailey. The contest featured players Dick Sisler, Lou Klein, Babe Martin, Joe Garagiola, and Yogi Berra. The major-leaguers won handily, 15-3.

Kinder never failed to amaze his younger teammates with his durability on the mound. "The main thing is to keep throwing every day, whether you've pitched yesterday or not," he said at age 40. He was later converted into a reliever, one of the first pitchers to do so successfully, and compiled 102 saves, the best record for any reliever between 1946 and 1960. But age eventually caught up with him and he was released by his last team in 1957 at age 42. "Once you get around the 40 mark, the officials completely lose sight of your abilities," he lamented. "All they notice is your age." Kinder died following heart surgery in Jackson in 1968.

THE 1940 GENERALS. LEFT TO RIGHT (TOP ROW): HARTLE GILLAND, CHARLES MARTIN, AL CUOZZO, ELLIS KINDER, NEWT "GASHOUSE" PARKER, CHARLEY GRAVES, CARL GAISER, MEL REIST, SHALER "PREACHER" GILLAND. BOTTOM ROW: MICKEY O'NEIL, ERNEST ANKROM, MEL MERKEL, JOE POLCHA, DICK JONES, EARL GRIFFITH, HARRY WILLIAMS. FOREGROUND: BATBOY FRED BAKER (RIGHT).

of baseball that Jackson fans will like." To fulfill this commitment, O'Neil completely purged the Generals' roster, with Jesse Webb, Ellis Kinder, Dick Jones, and Carl Gaiser the only survivors. He brought with him his own network of scouts and baseball contacts that searched for talent throughout the Ohio Valley and New York City area. The result was a young, hustling ballclub built on pitching, speed, and—a trait not seen on previous Jackson teams—power hitting.

Mickey O'Neil's presence helped bring a renewed enthusiasm for the Generals among local fans and led to the creation of the "Generals' Boosters," who proclaimed: "A boost for the Generals is a boost for Jackson." Its members spread throughout the city selling $1 buttons that allowed admission to the team's season opener. The Jackson Transportation Company, which before had never run city buses as far south as Bemis, offered trips from downtown to Lakeview Park and back. Even owner Hartle Gilland was excited about the upcoming season. "In past seasons, we've had a few deadheads on the team who were interested only in that twice a month visit to my office when they get their pay," he remarked. "The ball club [now] is made up of a fine group of youngsters who love baseball, who want to go up, and who want to win…I think Jackson is going to be proud of their ball team this year."

The Generals began the season at Bowling Green on May 8 with veteran Jesse Webb on the mound. "I'll give 'em all I got," he said before the game. "I feel fine. I'm in good shape, and I think I'll be able to mow 'em down." The "Pride of Medina" struck out 12 Barons and his teammates out-hit them 10 to 9, but the Kentuckians prevailed with a 6-5 victory. The loss was nullified the next day by Kitty League president Ben F. Howard because Bowling Green had violated the rule against teams having more than three class players on their roster.

Starting with a clean slate, the Generals returned to Jackson for their home opener the next day. The Generals' Boosters set up a parade from downtown Jackson to Lakeview Park and the local high school band performed before the game. Mayor A.B. Foust, who warmed up for the event in the Generals' bullpen, threw the ceremonial first pitch to Deputy Marshal Fred Exum behind home plate. With the community behind them, they beat the Barons 5-3 as Ellis Kinder struck out 10 and gave up only five hits.

The victory sparked a five-game win streak that propelled the Generals into first place. On May 12, Webb had a no-hitter in the works for the first five innings, but lost it in the sixth on a routine ground ball to third base that struck the dirt infield and shot over Ernie Ankrom's head for a base hit. Jesse tried to pick the runner off first base, but sent the throw past Newt Parker instead and allowed him to score. The right-hander knuckled down the rest of the game for a one-hitter and a 4-1 victory. Kinder followed the next night with a four-hit shutout against the Paducah Indians, 7-0, and struck out 11. Pitching in his first professional game, southpaw Charley Graves showed some wildness with six walks and a wild pitch yet held a two-run lead and beat the Indians 6-4. The game was highlighted by "Gashouse" Parker's three-run homer, the first of the season at Lakeview Park, that gave them the lead.

A four-game losing skid dropped the Generals from atop the standings temporarily, but they rebounded with five consecutive victories that put them back in the lead. Their bats erupted against the Mayfield Browns to sweep their three-game series at Lakeview, scoring 12 runs in the first three innings off two Browns hurlers on May 19 alone. Three days later, the Generals came from behind in the sixth inning at Owensboro to beat the Oilers, 8-5.

ELLIS KINDER

The victory, together with the league-leading Union City Greyhounds' 5-1 loss to Mayfield, boosted them back into first place.

Great pitching by Kinder, Webb, and Gaiser and the offensive punch of Parker and New York natives Joe Polcha and Al Cuozzo kept the Generals in the league lead the rest of the first half. The team impressed major league scout Steve O'Rourke, who spent a week looking them over for the New York Yankees. He applauded them as a reflection of their manager's hard-nosed, hustling style, calling them "one of the most disciplined ball clubs I have ever seen," and praising them as "one of the best looking ball clubs I have seen in Class D baseball."

One player the Yankees scout had his eye on was Ellis Kinder. The Arkansas right-hander had an impressive rookie campaign the year before, but made even more strides in 1940 thanks to new manager Mickey O'Neil. During spring training, the veteran catcher taught Kinder how to throw a fast-breaking curve rather than the slow, round-house one he relied on the year before. The result was an even better sophomore season in which he went 21-9 with a league-leading 2.38 ERA and a record-setting 307 strikeouts and 29 complete games. "But if it hadn't been for Mickey, I'd probably spent the rest of my life in the Kitty League," Kinder remarked years later while playing for the Boston Red Sox. "As I look back now, it was Mickey who gave me the urge to stay with baseball and keep pitchin' until I made the big show." At the end of the season, Hartle Gilland sold his contract to the Yankees for $3,500.

Fellow hurler Jesse Webb rebounded from an uncharacteristic .500 season the year before with a record of 17-14, a 3.82 ERA, 228 strikeouts, and 25 complete games. Carl Gaiser's late-season relief work the previous year earned him a place in the starting rotation in 1940, where he went 16-11 with 24 complete games. Hard-throwing rookie left-hander Charley Graves contributed six victories.

Scrappy shortstop Dick Jones, nicknamed the "Gilland's Gift to the Gals" for his boyish good looks, led the team in hitting for the second straight season, batting .338 with 35 doubles and leading the league in stolen bases for the second consecutive year with 51. Left fielder Al Cuozzo hit .307 with 11 home runs, 12 triples, and 71 RBI. Center fielder Joe Polcha, who played professional basketball for three years, combined speed with power to become the first 20-20 player in team history. He tied for the club lead in home runs (27) and was second in stolen bases (36) while hitting .292 with 97 RBIs. Newt "Gashouse" Parker, Jackson's 6' 3" 225-pound first baseman, tied Polcha for homers and led the team with 109 RBIs and the league with 128 strikeouts. Mickey O'Neil hit a steady .291 with 35 RBIs as the starting catcher.

JOE POLCHA

The hard-hitting Generals offense really cut into the profits of local restaurant owner Sam Bergel. Before the season began, he offered a free steak to every player who hit a triple or a home run. If he kept his promise, he helped stretch several players' meal allowances with 137 steak dinners on the house.

The Generals added more punch to their lineup in late June with the return of Melvin Merkel, who had been with the team two years earlier. The former first baseman was moved to right field and hit a two-run homer over the right field fence in his season debut on June 27. The Generals clinched the first-half pennant a week later with their 4-2 victory at Hopkinsville, finishing with a 38-23 record, 1½ games ahead of Paducah.

As the first half champions, Jackson hosted the annual Kitty League All-Star Game on July 9. Rather than use one of his veteran pitchers, Mickey O'Neil chose rookie Walter Callahan as his starter. The New York native hastened his departure by walking the first three hitters he faced and was taken out for another freshman hurler, the erratic Charley Graves. The lanky left-hander pitched out of the jam and held the All-Stars scoreless for the first two innings. A solo homer by Al Cuozzo gave the Generals the first run of the game.

> **Generals Fact**
> In the off-season, Generals outfielder Joe Polcha played in the American Basketball League (forerunner of the modern NBA). Between 1937 and 1941, Joe played for Brooklyn, Troy, and Baltimore.

Graves pitched himself into his own predicament in the third when he gave up three consecutive hits to load the bases, then hit Hopkinsville first baseman James Walker with a pitch to force in the All-Stars' first run that tied the score. He then issued three straight walks to bring in three more runs and give the All-Stars a 4-1 lead. The Jackson manager relieved him with yet another rookie, Jimmy Gates, who promptly walked the first batter he faced to force in yet another unearned run. Former General and Fulton manager Vincent "Moon" Mullen flew out to right field for the first out of the inning, but Gates walked the next batter to score another run. Owensboro slugger Eddie Urbon finally ended the charade with a grand slam homer that cleared the bases and gave the All-Stars an 11-1 lead. Without the worry of runners on the basepaths, Gates managed to strike out the next two batters to end the inning.

The Kitty League's best scored four more runs in the fourth, with Urbon smashing another home run to drive in seven runs in the contest. In the fifth inning, O'Neil finally chose experience over youth and brought in Jesse Webb to curb the All-Stars' scoring habit. Except for an unearned run in the frame, the veteran allowed only one hit and held them scoreless the remainder of the game. Despite Earl Griffith's RBI double in the fourth, Mel Merkel's solo homer in the fifth, and Al Cuozzo's 3-for-4 performance, the Generals could not generate enough offense against the All-Star hurlers and lost 11-4.

The second half pennant chase started with Carl Gaiser's two-hit, 3-2 victory over Fulton on July 10. Two errors in the ninth accounted for the unearned runs. A five-game losing streak July 18-22 dropped the Generals into fourth place, two games under .500. The last game, an 8-0 shutout against Owensboro, saw a bench-clearing brawl after a collision at home plate. In the sixth inning, Al Cuozzo threw a bullet from left field to catch Oilers pitcher Bud Sly attempting to score on a sacrifice fly. He collided hard into catcher Mickey O'Neil and a fight quickly erupted. It took members of the Jackson police to finally break it up.

After the brawl, the Generals rebounded by winning nine of their next 11 games, including a three-game sweep over the first-place Paduach Indians, to tie them for the league lead. Carl Gaiser twirled a three-hit, 1-0 shutout and struck out 12 in the first game on August 1 and back-to-back home runs by Joe Polcha and "Gashouse" Parker highlighted Jackson's 16-hit, 13-4 victory the next evening. While ace Ellis Kinder held Paducah to only four hits and fanned 14 batters, his teammates belted 23 hits in the 14-0 onslaught on August 3. Hard-hitting outfielders Al Cuozzo and Joe Polcha each had two homers, with Cuozzo knocking a grand slam over the right field fence in the first inning as part of his 5-for-5 performance.

Generals Fact
The Generals had 23 hits as Ellis Kinder shut out the first-place Paducah Indians for a four-hit, 14-0 victory on Aug. 3. Al Cuozzo went 5-for-5 with a grand slam.

A disastrous nine-game losing skid followed, however, dropping them into sixth place and the second division the rest of the season. Not even Ellis Kinder's five-hit, 16-strikeout performance against the Mayfield Browns on August 30 could win one for the Generals as they still managed to lose 1-0.

Illnesses, injuries, and an overworked pitching staff contributed to the team's late-season downfall. In late August, Jesse Webb contracted malaria during a series at Paducah and was out of action for several days. (This marked the third straight season that a Jackson player returned from a Paducah road series with malaria.) A chronically infected foot had Al Cuozzo in and out of the lineup while an illness kept Dick Jones out for a few days. O'Neil shuffled his lineup to compensate, moving center fielder Joe Polcha to third base while utility infielder Ernie Ankrom took over for Jones at short; Cuozzo (when available) was shifted from left to center; and newly acquired pitcher Harry Williams, who was signed to bolster the pitching staff, was forced into service in left field. The situation worsened when an Ellis Kinder fastball fractured O'Neil's thumb, forcing him to manage from the bench the remainder of the season. Ankrom was drafted as his backstop replacement and Williams was moved to third base, allowing Polcha to return to the outfield. Ironically, the injury occurred on "Mickey O'Neil Night" at Lakeview Park as the Generals honored him for winning the first-half pennant.

The day before the season ended, Mickey O'Neil, club president Hartle Gilland, and Harry Williams as well as the manager and owner of the Hopkinsville Hoppers were called to Chicago by Commissioner Kenesaw Mountain Landis. He questioned them regarding an allegation made by Owensboro manager Hugh Wise that both clubs intentionally lost their recent games with first-place Bowling Green to help the Barons win the second-half pennant. Wise cited Jackson's 14-6 loss on September 3 in which O'Neil used Al Cuozzo as his starting pitcher and later brought in Williams from the outfield as a reliever. O'Neil and Gilland explained the unusual switch due to the team's crippled situation to the satisfaction of Judge Landis and the matter was dropped.

JUDGE KENESAW MOUNTAIN LANDIS

The Generals lost seven of their last 10 games to end the second half in fifth place with a record of 29-32, 10 games behind Bowling Green, and the season with an overall record of 66-58. But their first-half pennant still enabled them to face the second-half champion Barons in a best-of-seven championship series with a reported $5,000 at stake. The league allowed them two additions to their postseason roster: Hopkinsville manager Charles Martin to replace the injured Mickey O'Neil behind the plate and outfielder Mel Reist to take over for Al Cuozzo.

The first two games of the series were played at Lakeview Park. The Barons took a three-run lead in the opener on September 10 against starter Jesse Webb, but the Generals scored a run in the fourth on Ernie Ankrom's RBI double and two more in the following frame. In the sixth, Joe Polcha hit a single with two outs to score Mel Merkel on the left fielder's error and give them the lead. With Polcha on third, Barons hurler Elmer Haas walked "Gashouse" Parker, who then faked a steal of second to draw the catcher's throw. The Barons' receiver took Haas' next pitch and rushed toward the big first sacker, who stood halfway between the two bases before slowly going toward second. The decoy enabled the speedy Polcha to score before Parker was tagged for the third out. Parker's two-run homer in the seventh sealed the victory, 7-4, even though the ball had lodged at the top of the left field fence instead of leaving the park.

But the Barons' hitting habit, especially in the early innings, was too much for Jackson's pitching staff and the Generals dropped the next three games. Just one loss away from elimination, they fought back to win the next two and tie the series. In the seventh and deciding game, Carl Gaiser held Bowling Green's bats in check for eight scattered hits, though he gave up six free passes and had no strikeouts. Polcha broke out of his series hitting slump with a double in the first inning that scored Merkel for Jackson's first run and was driven home on Mel Reist's single. "Gashouse" Parker's fourth-inning double scored Polcha to give them a 3-1 lead, enabling the Generals to take the final game, 4-2, and the postseason series.

Despite their come-from-behind victory over the second-half champions, league officials declared Bowling Green the league champions based on their overall season record. Regardless, the victorious Generals were given a farewell party the next day by the Gillands at Lakeview Park in appreciation of their winning season.

1940 Kitty League Standings

First Half (May 8-July 8)

Team	W	L	Pct	GB
Jackson Generals	38	25	.603	—
Paducah Indians	36	28	.563	2.5
Bowling Greeb Barons	33	29	.532	4.5
Union City Greyhounds	34	30	.531	4.5
Owensboro Oilers	31	32	.492	7
Mayfield Browns	31	32	.492	7
Fulton Tigers	29	34	.460	9
Hopkinsville Hoppers	21	43	.328	17.5

Second Half (July 10-September 8)

Team	W	L	Pct	GB
Bowling Green Barons	41	21	.661	—
Paducah Indians	40	23	.635	1.5
Owensboro Oilers	38	25	.603	3.5
Mayfield Browns	36	27	.571	5.5
Jackson Generals	**29**	**32**	**.473**	**11.5**
Union City Greyhounds	25	36	.410	15.5
Fulton Tigers	25	39	.391	17
Hopkinsville Hoppers	14	45	.237	25.5

Split-season playoff—Jackson beat Bowling Green 4 games to 3, but the Barons were named league champions based on their full-season record.

1941

Finish	Record	Pct.	GB
First	(84-43)	.661	—

Manager	Record	Pct.
George (Mickey) O'Neil	(84-43)	.661

Attendance	Lg Rank
Not available	

Future and Former Major Leaguers
Ellis Kinder
Mickey O'Neil

Starting Lineup
C	Mickey O'Neil	.248 BA
1B	Melvin (Mel) Merkel	.333 BA
2B	Lloyd Maloney	.286 BA
3B	Ernest (Ernie) Ankrom	.285 BA
SS	Wallace (Wally) Noon	.311 BA
LF	Al Cuozzo	.349 BA
CF	Andy Scarbola	.297 BA
RF	Mel Reist	.323 BA

Pitching Staff
RH	Carl Gaiser	(26-5)
RH	Jesse Webb	(25-6)
RH	Ellis Kinder	(11-6)
LH	Charley Graves	(11-10)
LH	Leonard (Len) Hornsby	(8-10)

Top 10 Batters and Top 5 Pitchers

Batter	BA	G	AB	R	H	2B	3B	HR	RBI	SB
Gashouse Parker	.405	20	74	30	30	7	0	16	37	2
Al Cuozzo	.349	97	416	74	145	27	8	23	99	9
Melvin Merkel	.333	126	481	116	160	30	5	30	100	24
Mel Reist*	.323	120	471	87	152	31	6	10	99	33
Wallace Noon	.311	126	540	121	168	41	7	8	65	7
Andy Scarbola	.297	104	394	73	117	23	3	12	63	27
Lloyd Maloney	.286	125	521	105	149	30	4	4	44	6
Ernest Ankrom	.285	121	460	77	131	46	3	12	85	11
Ray Haynes	.263	66	237	31	62	11	3	0	34	6
Mickey O'Neil	.248	69	222	24	55	10	1	0	31	10

Pitcher	ERA	G	IP	W	L	CG	ER	Sh	BB	SO
Ellis Kinder	2.88	18	153	11	6	17	49	—	47	179
Jesse Webb	3.08	33	260	25	6	23	88	—	79	248
Carl Gaiser	3.11	32	275	26	5	26	95	—	75	205
Leonard Hornsby	4.11	29	118	8	10	4	54	—	64	79
Charley Graves	4.71	33	212	11	10	13	111	—	106	151

*Also with the Hopkinsville Hoppers

The Jackson Generals entered the 1941 season as the favorites to win the Kitty League pennant. Despite the loss of powerful center fielder Joe Polcha to the nation's first peacetime military draft and 21-game winner Ellis Kinder's sale to the New York Yankees organization, the team offense and pitching staff were still formidable and the Gillands had managed to retain most of the championship club from the previous season. "Jackson has the most experienced ball club in the league," Fulton manager and former Generals skipper "Moon" Mullen believed. "They should be sitting at the top of the loop."

Some 2,000 fans attended the season opener at Lakeview Park on May 11 against the Union City Greyhounds. The Jackson High School band played the National Anthem and entertained the packed grandstand with "Take Me Out to the Ballgame." City commissioner Perry H. Callahan threw the first pitch to catcher and city engineer John Gasell, but Madison County Sheriff and batter Ewing Griffin connected for a ground ball to second baseman Lloyd Maloney to start the season. The game was tied 1-1 in the eighth before Maloney connected for a solo homer to give Jackson the lead. Two batters later, "Gashouse" Parker added a two-run blast to give starting pitcher Carl Gaiser the victory, 4-2. In his season debut, veteran right-hander Jesse Webb struck out 17 Greyhounds at Union City three days later and, though he gave up 11 hits, still managed to fashion a 1-0 shutout. Jackson swept a three-game series at Bowling Green and won their first game from the Fulton Tigers (now a farm club of the Detroit Tigers) to jump into first place.

But the Generals dropped their next six games and fell into fourth place. The last game, a 6-3 loss to Hopkinsville, ended with scrappy team captain Ernie Ankrom running out a ground ball and colliding with Hoppers manager Chet "Wimpy" Wilburn covering first base. The two quickly came to blows and both benches rushed onto the field. The free-for-all lasted several minutes before Tennessee Highway Patrolmen were able to separate the combatants. One unnamed player who chose to remain on the Generals' bench during the fight later received a busted lip in the clubhouse courtesy of manager Mickey O'Neil for not helping his teammates.

The fight proved to be just the spark that the Generals needed to get back on the winning track. They won 11 of their next 15 games and were back in first place to stay. Five home runs against Bowling Green highlighted an 18-hit attack on May 28. Shortstop Wally Noon, who replaced veteran Dick Jones after his sale to the Jackson, Mississippi club of the Southeastern League, started the barrage with an inside-the-park homer in the first inning. Al Cuozzo and "Gashouse" Parker each had two round-trippers, with Cuozzo belting a grand slam in the fifth inning. The onslaught gave lefty Charley Graves plenty of cushion as he held the Barons to four hits and struck out 14. His 16-2 victory put Jackson back at the top of the standings.

Carl Gaiser surprised the entire Kitty League with his remarkable and record-breaking performance during the season. Expected to be the number two hurler behind veteran Jesse Webb on the Generals' staff, the Bloomington,

CARL GAISER

Illinois right-hander became its ace, winning 14 consecutive starts en route to accumulating the most victories in a single season in league history. "Gaiser is tall and pitches with the most beautiful form in the league," *Sun* sports editor James Goodwin wrote. "He has style. He has plenty of speed, a nice breaking curve, and fields his position better than an average pitcher." Gaiser compensated for his lack of an overpowering fastball with a good curve, using a sidearm delivery and a quick release to fool hitters. His fastball "couldn't break a window pane," remembered Generals batboy Fred Baker, "but he knew how to throw. He could get the ball over the plate." He also displayed great control, walking only 75 batters in 275 innings pitched.

The Generals lost their biggest bat at the end of May when Newt Parker, who had been sold in the off-season to Tulsa, Oklahoma of the Texas League but optioned back to Jackson, was recalled by Tulsa and assigned to the Hutchinson, Kansas club of the Class C Western Association. The big man had been on a big tear, hitting 16 homers in his first 20 games and driving in 37 runs at a .405 clip. Going to a higher classification was a step closer to the major leagues, but he still regretted it. "I hate to leave here hitting like I am," Parker said at the time. "I want a shot at the home run record in the Kitty." But he did give Jackson fans a memorable farewell in the Generals' Memorial Day doubleheader against Bowling Green on May 30. "Gashouse" smashed two homers in the first game and two in the second, driving in seven runs in the twin victories. The four round-trippers in his final two games gave him seven total against the Barons in the four-game series. He later recalled that day as the most memorable of his professional career.

Newt "Gashouse" Parker

Generals Fact
Generals first baseman William Newton "Gashouse" Parker hit 16 home runs in the first 20 games of the 1941 season.

As it turned out, Hutchinson had Parker's bat for only three games before he was notified of his impending induction into the Army. After his discharge following World War II, he managed a minor league club in his hometown of LaGrange, Georgia and was reunited later in the season with former Generals Mickey O'Neil, Mel Merkel, and Andy Scarbola at Leaksville, North Carolina, a farm club of the Pittsburgh Pirates. "Gashouse" played at least seven more years, managing teams at Edenton and Hickory toward the end of his career.

With Parker's departure, O'Neil shifted Mel Merkel to first base and acquired outfielder Mel Reist, who had played with the Generals during the 1940 postseason, from Hopkinsville for pitcher Normand Southard. Reist added more speed to the lineup, stealing 33 bases while hitting .323 with 10 home runs and 99 RBIs with both clubs. He was also the team's best defensive outfielder, committing only eight errors with a .970 fielding percentage.

The power void in the Generals' lineup left by "Gashouse" Parker was quickly filled by

MEL MERKEL

Al Cuozzo and Mel Merkel. Cuozzo overtook Parker's home run and RBI totals and led the league for most of the season in both categories before illness forced him out of the lineup for several weeks, limiting him to 97 games. He finished third in the league with 23 homers and 99 RBIs while leading Jackson in hitting at .349. Merkel passed his teammate on August 17 for a league-leading 30 homers with 100 RBIs to lead the team. He was just six stolen bases shy of becoming the only General in franchise history with 30 homers and 30 stolen bases in the same season.

Although he lacked Dick Jones' exceptional speed on the basepaths, "Wally" Noon proved to be a good hitter, leading the team with 168 hits and 121 runs scored while hitting .311 in the leadoff spot. Fellow Ohio native Lloyd Maloney contributed a steady .286 average at second base. Andy Scarbola, who replaced fellow New Yorker Joe Polcha in center field, paced the team with 27 stolen bases while batting .297 with 12 homers and 63 RBIs. Team captain Ernie Ankrom, the Generals' versatile utility player in 1940, was rewarded with regular play at third base and contributed 12 homers and 85 RBIs.

As if the trio of Carl Gaiser, Jesse Webb, and Charley Graves weren't enough to worry Kitty League hitters, the Generals' pitching staff was further strengthened in mid-June with the return of Ellis Kinder. According to Jackson *Sun* sports editor James Goodwin, Kinder's contract had been sold to the Yankees for $3,500, half of which was paid at the end of the 1940 season and the rest owed after the first month of the 1941 season. In May, the New York front office claimed Kinder had developed a sore arm and asked for an additional 30 days to complete the sale. But at the end of the extension, they wanted to renegotiate the price entirely and the Generals simply asked for their prize prospect back. It was later suggested that the real reason the Yankees did not purchase Kinder's contract was his reputation as a hard drinker and feared his influence on their young, impressionable prospects. In his first game back on June 15, the Arkansas right-hander set Paducah down on two hits before a sellout crowd at Lakeview Park as his teammates walloped two Indian hurlers with 12 hits in a 12-6 victory. He won his next six games and ended the season at 11-6, leading the team with a 2.88 ERA (seventh in the league) and pitching 17 complete games in 18 starts.

By virtue of their first place standing on July 4, Jackson hosted the All-Star Game for the second consecutive year. This time Mickey O'Neil took no chances on rookie hurlers, going with "Old Faithful," Jesse Webb, as his starter. But the veteran gave up six runs on five hits in the first two innings and had to be relieved by Carl Gaiser. The league's winningest pitcher gave up a home run to Hopkinsville's Tony Kvedar in the fifth that added to the All-Stars' lead. Ellis Kinder shut down their offense in the last two frames, but Jackson lost 7-2.

The Generals continued their dominance of the Kitty League in the second half. From May 26 (their first win after "The Fight") until the end of the season, they did not lose more

The 1941 Kitty League champions. Left to right (top row): Andy Scarbola, Charley Graves, Carl Gaiser, Ellis Kinder, Wallace Noon, Mel Reist, Mel Merkel. Bottow row: Al Cuozzo, Jesse Webb, Ernie Ankrom, Mickey O'Neil, Len Hornsby, Ray Haynes, Lloyd Maloney.

than two games in a row. A 12-game winning streak July 17-28 further cemented their hold on first place. During the streak, Kinder held the Oilers to three hits at Owensboro in their 5-3 victory. It ended at Bowling Green when Kinder, who had a shutout going into the ninth inning, gave up a bases-loaded single in the thirteenth to give the Barons a 4-3 decision.

The most one-sided affair of the season was the Generals' 22-0 route over Hopkinsville on August 6. As Jesse Webb offered his encouragement from the third base coach's box, his teammates shelled the Hopper hurlers with 21 hits. Mickey O'Neil, Andy Scarbola, Ernie Ankrom, and Wally Noon each drove in three runs and Noon and Al Cuozzo hit home runs. Kinder hurled a three-hitter for his seventh win in nine starts, striking out 10 and walking only one.

One month later, Jackson was involved in another high scoring, though more competitive, contest with another Kentucky rival. Bowling Green's starting pitcher was bombarded for nine runs in

> **Generals Fact**
> The most one-sided game of the season was the Generals' 22-0 victory over the Hopkinsville Hoppers on August 6.

the first inning alone on September 6 and was scored upon in every frame but two. Generals starter Casie Vinson was driven from the mound himself after the fourth, giving up nine runs on eight hits, nine walks, and a balk. Rather than waste one of his other starters, O'Neil sent outfielder Mel Reist to the hill. The converted hurler certainly did no worse than his predecessor, allowing seven runs on nine hits while striking out seven and walking two. At the plate he went four-for-six, sending two home runs out of Lakeview Park and driving in six runs. Wally Noon led the team with his six-for-seven performance, hitting two doubles, scoring four times, and driving in four runs. In all, there were 42 hits in the contest, 25 belonging to Jackson. The Generals won the free-scoring battle, 21-16.

Manager Mickey O'Neil suffered a season-ending injury for the second straight year when he broke his left leg on August 26. Again the injury took place on a night held in his honor at Lakeview Park. Shortstop Wally Noon took over as the starting catcher until he injured his finger on a foul tip four days later. He was replaced by third sacker Ernie Ankrom, who also took over leadership of the club on road trips. O'Neil was forced to manage from the dugout the rest of the season, but his injury didn't prevent him from arguing with the umpire on occasion. "But this time he bounced out of the dugout like a human pogo stick," recalled Generals fan John D. Graham. "His entire leg was encased in plaster of paris, but the turbulent skipper moved faster than most men could with two good legs."

During an August 28 contest against Union City, Generals owner Hartle Gilland announced that the next Jackson batter who hit a home run would receive a $25 Defense Bond. Light-hitting pitcher Jesse Webb, who had never lifted one out of the park in his professional career, almost poked one over the right field fence. Four days later, Al Cuozzo belted his 18th round-tripper of the season in the first inning to win it.

It was only appropriate that Carl Gaiser, who started and won the first game of the season for the Generals, take the mound for their last game on September 12. After three straight losses, he was tied with teammate Jesse Webb at 25 wins, just one shy of claiming the Kitty League record for victories in a season. Slugger Mel Merkel did his part, belting his 29th and 30th home runs of the season and driving in seven runs (the most ever by a General in one game) to claim the league's home run crown. Gaiser held the Hoppers to five hits and struck out nine for an 11-5 victory to clinch the mark with a record of 26-5. The Generals finished at 84-43, a comfortable 14½ games ahead of second-place Hopkinsville, to become the first and only Jackson team to win the Kitty League pennant. Their lead was the third highest of any championship club in league history.

Generals Fact
At the time, the Generals' .661 winning percentage was the best in Kitty League history.

The Generals faced their season-long rivals, the fourth-place Mayfield Browns, in the Shaughnessy playoffs. It promised to be an interesting showdown: both teams had taken nine games from the other during the season, with the Kentuckians winning their last five encounters. Mayfield was the best hitting club in the league at .287, just two points ahead of Jackson, but the Generals had the edge in pitching and batting power.

The best-of-five series opened at Lakeview Park on September 14. Mayfield's pitching was shaky, with starter Ray Minor giving 10 free passes in six-and-a-third inning's work. Al Cuozzo's three-run clout off reliever Paul Henderson highlighted a seven-run rally in the seventh that won the first game, 12-5. The next evening, Jesse Webb held the Browns scoreless through the first five innings and led 4-0, but gave up seven runs in the next three to force his early exit. Carl Gaiser took over in the ninth, only to surrender a grand slam home run to Mayfield manager Mickey Hornsby and drop the second game, 11-6. Club president Hartle Gilland treated the players and their families to a post-game barbecue at the ballpark in celebration of their pennant-winning season. Mickey O'Neil was given a wrist watch by the players and each received a gold baseball inscribed: "Kitty League Champions of 1941."

The series moved to Mayfield on September 16. Despite giving up nine walks, pitcher Normand Southard limited his former teammates to one run before surrendering three in the ninth. With the bases loaded and no outs, reliever Paul Henderson was brought in and, though he gave up a run himself, preserved the Browns' second win of the series, 7-5. Only one loss away from elimination, O'Neil gave the ball to Ellis Kinder, who turned in a seven-hit performance, striking out seven and walking two. The right-hander made only two mistakes, each coming off the bat of third baseman Dick Kimble, who sent two of his offerings over the right field fence for the Kentuckians' three runs. Meanwhile the Generals' offense was smothered by Claude Drye, who avenged his early exit in the second game with a three-hit shutout that closed the book on Jackson's championship season.

1941 Kitty League Standings

Team	W	L	PCT	GB
Jackson Generals	84	43	.661	—
Hopkinsville Hoppers	69	57	.548	14.5
Fulton Tigers	68	59	.535	16
Mayfield Browns	64	63	.504	20
Union City Greyhounds	62	64	.492	21.5
Owensboro Oilers	58	68	.460	25.5
Bowling Green Barons	55	71	.437	28.5
Paducah Indians	46	81	.362	38

Shaughnessy playoffs—Mayfield beat Jackson 3 games to 1 and Hopkinsville beat Fulton 3 games to 2.

Finals—Mayfield beat Hopkinsville 4 games to 1

1942

Finish	Record	Pct.	GB
Third*	(29-19)	.604	3

*Kitty League disbanded on June 18

Manager	Record	Pct.
George (Mickey) O'Neil	(29-19)	.604

Attendance	Lg Rank
Not available	

Future and Former Major Leaguers
Ed Wright
Mickey O'Neil

Starting Lineup
C	Ocky Walls	.280 BA
1B	Ralph Smith	.262 BA
2B	Lloyd Maloney	.287 BA
3B	Ernest Ankrom	.335 BA
SS	Glen (Burper) Belcher	.317 BA
LF	Vincent Lepore	.349 BA
CF	Ray Riley	.274 BA
RF	Charles Reeder	.338 BA

Pitching Staff
LH	Leonard (Len) Hornsby	(6-7)
RH	Doyle Brady	(5-1)
RH	Jesse Webb	(5-4)
RH	Ed Wright	(4-0)
RH	Carl Gaiser	(4-4)

Top 10 Batters and Top 5 Pitchers

Batter	BA	G	AB	R	H	2B	3B	HR	RBI	SB
Vincent Lepore	.349	25	109	24	38	8	1	0	14	2
Charles Reeder	.338	20	74	15	25	5	0	1	13	1
Ernest Ankrom	.335	48	194	50	65	10	4	7	54	11
Glenn Belcher	.317	46	199	37	63	8	2	2	42	8
John Janze	.315	21	92	20	29	3	0	3	11	2
Leonard Hornsby	.303	30	65	17	20	4	3	1	8	3
Lloyd Maloney	.287	48	195	52	56	8	1	1	22	7
Ocky Walls	.280	48	164	25	46	11	0	0	28	1
Ray Riley	.274	47	190	39	52	9	3	3	32	17
Ralph Smith	.262	26	122	23	32	9	0	1	27	7

Pitcher	ERA	G	IP	W	L	CG	ER	Sh	BB	SO
Ed Wright	2.68	4	37	4	0	4	11	—	8	35
Carl Gaiser	3.12	13	85	4	4	6	39	—	23	50
Doug Brady	—	16	70	5	1	1	—	—	17	20
Jesse Webb	—	10	56	5	2	3	—	—	20	49

THE 1942 SEASON

The Kitty League was reduced to a six-club circuit in 1942. The American Legion post at Paducah dropped its sponsorship of the Indians when a proposed working agreement with the New York Giants fell through. To have a balanced circuit, the league was forced to drop the Mayfield Browns, even though they had already sold all their season tickets.

With the attack on Pearl Harbor on December 7, 1941, America was at war and many players from the Generals' pennant-winning season were fighting in it. But President Franklin D. Roosevelt wanted major and minor league baseball to continue and give the nation a diversion from the conflict. League president Shelby Peace warned club owners before the season began of the impending hardships ahead of them, including a government-imposed restriction on using chartered buses for road trips after June 1 and a lack of quality players due to the draft. Nevertheless, the owners chose to play out the season.

The war claimed most of the Generals' roster from the 1941 season. Team captain Ernie Ankrom was one of the few returning veterans, along with second baseman Lloyd Maloney and pitchers Leonard "Len" Hornsby and Jesse Webb (though he staged a three-week contract holdout during spring training). The rest of the club was filled with rookies uncovered by Mickey O'Neil's scouting network. Ralph Smith took over at first base and Glen Belcher (nicknamed "Burper" by his teammates) at short, with veterans Maloney at second and Ankrom at third. The outfield was patrolled by youngsters Ray Grissom in left, Ray Riley in center, and John Janse in right. O'Neil chose to manage from the dugout rather than behind the plate as Georgia semi-pro Ocky Walls took over as the starting catcher. Jesse Webb returned for his eighth season with the Generals. Left-handers Len Hornsby and Bucky Scolpini and rookie right-handers Doyle Brady, John Mueller, and Tony Sheanshang filled out the staff.

The 1942 Generals were a younger, faster, though less powerful team than those of the last two seasons. Local sports editor James Goodwin justified the changes, believing that "everybody and all got tired of home runs" in 1941 as they took "the biggest thrill out of baseball by making home runs commonplace events." Jackson fans certainly saw less of the long ball as the Generals dropped from first in the league in homers in '41 to third in the six-club circuit in '42. But it was still the best hitting club in the Kitty with a .286 batting average, leading the league in total bases (669) and stolen bases (72). Defensively, they were second with a .946 fielding percentage.

Three-year veteran Ernie Ankrom led the team's offensive attack, batting .335 in 48 games while leading the league with seven homers and the team with 54 RBIs. "Burper" Belcher finished second in the Generals'

LADIES NIGHT

Tonight, May 5
Ladies Free

All ladies will be admitted free to the game tonight whether accompanied by gentlemen or not. Come on out and see the game as guest of Lakeview.

BOWLING GREEN
Vs.
JACKSON GENERALS

8:15   LAKEVIEW

batting race at .317 with 42 RBIs, followed by John Janse at .315. Cincinnati native Ray Riley, whom Mickey O'Neil felt was a better defensive outfielder than Mel Reist, was the club's stolen base leader with 17 while hitting .274 with 32 RBIs.

Southpaw Len Hornsby led the pitching staff in victories with his 6-7 record and 55 strikeouts. Jesse Webb and Doug Brady tied for second with five wins each, "Old Faithful" finishing at 5-2 with 49 strikeouts and Brady winning his first three games for a 5-1 mark. Carl Gaiser was 4-2 after returning to the team and tied Hornsby in complete games at five each. Right-hander Ed Wright, who had a brief stint with the Generals four years earlier before he was sidelined with an appendicitis, had the most impressive performance of the season. He won all four of his starts after being optioned to the Generals from the Memphis Chicks and had a 2.68 ERA, fifth best in the league. Three years later, the Dyersburg, Tennessee native posted an 8-3 record and 2.51 ERA for the Boston Braves. He spent the next four seasons with the Braves and one with the Philadelphia Athletics, finishing his major league career with a record of 25-16.

> **Generals Fact**
> Rookie shortstop Glen Belcher—nicknamed "Burper" by his teammates—went 7-for-7 at the plate in a Memorial Day doubleheader.

Four games into the season, the Generals took possession of third place but could not get past Fulton or Bowling Green to climb any higher. Jesse Webb began the season in typical fashion, hurling a no-hitter into the fifth inning on May 10 but settling for a four-hitter against the Union City Greyhounds. He struck out 10 and walked only one for a 13-2 victory. Cleanup hitter Ralph Smith's 4-for-5 performance, with three doubles and four RBI, led Jackson's 18-hit attack. Ernie Ankrom had three hits and drove in five runs. Shortstop Glen Belcher, continuing the tradition of great individual performances in the Memorial Day doubleheader, was a perfect 7-for-7 at the plate in both contests with three stolen bases and three runs batted in.

The Generals went on a tear in June, winning 13 of the last 18 games of the shortened season. From June 6-13 they won nine consecutive games, the last three against first-place Fulton. The streak began with Jackson's 9-5 victory over Union City, during which starter Jesse Webb, while backing up a play at third base, was nailed in the face by second baseman Lloyd Maloney's wild throw. Jesse came out of the game but returned to the mound black-and-blue four days later to get his fifth win. Despite their winning outburst, the team could only get as close as 1½ games of first and were still stuck in third place, one game behind Bowling Green.

Amid rumors that the Kitty League would soon fold, the Generals played their last game at Lakeview Park on June 16. They dropped the first game of the doubleheader, 13-2, but right-hander Ed Wright came through with a four-hitter in the second, striking out 10 and walking none for a 5-2 win.

The rumors proved to be true. The Union City ownership had been among the strongest supporters to go forward with the season, but a 9-35 record and a $3,500 loss forced the St. Louis Cardinals farm club to disband. At the same time, the Bowling Green Barons lost their sponsorship from the local American Legion post and the Owensboro Oilers, having lost money themselves, looked as if they would share the same fate. Jackson, Fulton, Owensboro, and Hopkinsville hoped to continue with a four-club circuit, but the Detroit Tigers rebuffed the idea and withdrew its working agreement with Fulton, forcing its disbandment.

THE 1942 SEASON

The Generals' last game of the season was a 7-4 loss at Bowling Green, highlighted by home runs off the bats of Ernie Ankrom and Glen Belcher. Jackson finished in third place with a record of 29-18, three games behind the champion Fulton Tigers. Their top players were quickly sold to other minor league clubs: Carl Gaiser, Ernie Ankrom, and Lloyd Maloney went to the Richmond Blues of the Piedmont League and Lynn Hornsby and Glen Belcher to Anniston, Alabama of the Southeastern League. Manager Mickey O'Neil accepted the skipper's position with the Three Rivers club of the Canadian-American League. Team owner Hartle Gilland went out of the baseball business and converted the Lakeview Park grandstand into The Pit Cafe and Steak House that operated for several years.

1942 Kitty League Standings

Team	W	L	Pct	GB
Fulton Tigers	30	14	.682	—
Bowling Green Barons	31	15	.674	1
Jackson Generals	29	19	.604	3
Hopkinsville Hoppers	23	23	.500	8
Owensboro Oilers	16	32	.333	17
Union City Greyhounds	9	35	.205	21

Kitty League disbanded on June 18

Jesse Webb's Last Season

Jesse Webb pitched his last game for the Generals in the afternoon tilt of a doubleheader on June 16, 1942. He was driven from the mound with only one out in the first inning, giving up seven runs on five hits, walking two and striking out one. When the Kitty League folded, it was rumored that he would follow manager Mickey O'Neil to the Canadian-American League. Instead, he returned to his farm near Medina, Tennessee and pitched occasionally for area semi-pro teams.

In 1946, the Kitty League returned and the Union City Greyhounds, languishing in the second division of the standings, was desperate for pitching help. Having already turned down the Fulton Chicks that spring—he needed to plant his crops, he told them—Jesse signed with Union City because it was the closest team to his home.

At 36 years old, Webb had lost some speed on his fastball and his stamina wasn't what it once was. But as usual, he claimed to be in the best shape of his life. One fan shouted to him from the stands, "You still as fast as ever?" Webb simply made a downward, arching motion with his hand, indicating that he wasn't what he used to be. But after the first inning, he came back to the dugout and told his younger teammates, "I feel fine. Think I'll pitch again tomorrow." His best performace of the 1946 season was a four-hitter against the Mayfield Clothiers, striking out 10 batters and walking only one for a 3-2 win. Jesse contributed a 6-5 record and 3.73 ERA for the seventh-place Greyhounds and finished second on the pitching staff with 79 strikeouts.

Jesse even took a shot at managing the club the last two weeks of the season—"Sorta holdin' the club together," he called it. He shared the responsibility with second baseman Bill Sweatt. Asked how he liked the job, he said, "It's all right, I guess. But it all depends on what you've got to manage. When you don't have as good a ball club as the other teams, you can't do much managing."

One facet of the job he didn't care for was confronting the umpire. During one game, his partner disputed a hit batsman call by umpire John Henry Suther but wasn't making any progress. Looking for backup, he called into the dugout, "Hey, Jesse! Come here!" But Webb hid further in its shadows. "Maybe he forgot that he was the boss now," offered one sportswriter. Or maybe Jesse knew better than to challenge Suther, a former All-American football player who had punched a teammate back in 1935.

1950

Finish	Record	Pct.	GB
Third	(68-52)	.567	6

Manager	Record	Pct.
Glen (Gabby) Stewart	(68-52)	.567

Attendance	Lg Rank
30,078	Fourth

Former Major Leaguers
Glen (Gabby) Stewart

Starting Lineup

C	Glen (Gabby) Stewart	.346 BA
1B	Dominic Italiano	.247 BA
2B	Bearl Brooks	.238 BA
3B	Emil Kirik	.268 BA
SS	Clyde Barger	.224 BA
LF	Harold (Hal) Seawright	.317 BA
CF	Maurice Partain	.299 BA
RF	Robert Samaras	.268 BA

Pitching Staff

RH	Walt Mestan	(16-5)
LH	Richard (Dick) Janasky	(15-9)
LH	Tillman (Mike) Conovan	(9-10)
LH	Robert (Bob) Evans	(6-6)
RH	Roy Walkup	(5-4)

Top 10 Batters and Top 5 Pitchers

Batter	BA	G	AB	R	H	2B	3B	HR	RBI	SB
Gabby Stewart	.346	98	364	63	126	38	2	2	82	11
Hal Seawright	.317	49	183	31	58	8	1	9	38	6
Maurice Partain	.299	119	476	113	138	23	1	3	61	83
Hayden Ray	.276	103	388	64	107	9	2	3	42	14
Bob Samaras	.268	73	261	39	70	13	6	7	50	6
Emil Kirik	.268	84	243	31	65	9	2	0	40	3
Lee Valadez	.259	120	406	77	105	11	1	1	54	23
Dominic Italiano	.247	119	377	77	93	17	1	2	57	15
Bearl Brooks	.238	83	315	50	75	6	3	0	37	16
Clyde Barger	.224	91	250	31	56	6	1	0	41	1

Pitcher	ERA	G	IP	W	L	CG	ER	Sh	BB	SO
Dick Janasky	3.38	28	181	15	9	13	67	5	46	130
Walt Mestan	3.43	26	173	16	5	12	66	3	88	118
Mike Conovan	3.86	24	133	9	10	10	57	0	26	107
Roy Walkup	4.10	22	101	5	4	4	46	0	64	52
Bill Chambers	—	12	93	5	5	10	—	2	37	54

There was renewed interest in bringing professional baseball back to Jackson in the spring of 1949. A major stumbling block was removed when local fan Charlie Williams led a successful referendum to permit Sunday baseball within the city limits. Five local businessmen Aaron Robinson, Sam Wahl, Harold Simpson, Russell Rice, and Irvin Freedman established the Jackson Baseball Association Incorporated to acquire a professional franchise for the city. Initially they pursued a club in the Class D Mississippi-Ohio Valley (MOV) League, but were discouraged by the great distance between Jackson and the other league cities. In June, Horace M. "Hod" Lisenbee, owner and manager of the Clarksville Colts, offered to sell them his struggling Kitty League franchise. It was believed that the Association purchased the club for less than the $17,000 asking price. The sale was announced on October 25 and the Kitty League approved it a week later.

The purchase of the Clarksville Colts included the players' contracts, uniforms, equipment, and the team bus. Rather than improve one of Jackson's existing ballparks, team officials chose instead to convert the racetrack at the Fairgrounds into a baseball diamond and use its expansive 4,000-seat grandstand, naming it Municipal Park. A scoreboard and outfield fences with advertisements were constructed and new lighting equipment was installed for night games. "Our ballpark is being equipped with the latest General Electric lighting system recommended for Class 'C' ball," executive secretary Russell Rice wrote the new players, "having 160 sealed-beam reflectors, the same as those used in the Polo Grounds."

Glen "Gabby" Stewart was signed as player-manager of the new Generals. The Tullahoma, Tennessee native made his major league debut with the New York Giants in 1940, hitting only .138 in 15 games. He returned to the majors three years later as a utility infielder with the wartime Philadelphia Phillies, but hit only .216 in two seasons. Before signing with Jackson, he had managed the Hot Springs, Arkansas club of the Cotton States League.

"Gabby" was given his nickname early in his career though he never really earned it. The 37-year-old veteran was a soft-spoken and easy-going manager who never raised his voice against his players or the umpires (at least in Jackson). If a player made a mistake, Gabby discussed it with him at his locker away from his teammates. All he asked was that they do their best and

Manager Glen "Gabby" Stewart

hustle. He was the team's best hitter during the season, batting .346 with 82 RBIs in 98 games. He preferred doubles more than any other extra-base hit and lead the Kitty League with 38. During the first week of June, he hit 11 doubles in a row.

Jackson was one of only three independent clubs in the Kitty League during the 1950 season. The others were the Union City Greyhounds and the Cairo (IL) Dodgers. The remaining five had working agreements with major or minor league teams: the Fulton Railroaders with the Washington Senators; the Mayfield Clothiers with the Pittsburgh Pirates; the Owensboro Oilers with the Boston Braves; the Madisonville (KY) Miners with the Chicago White Sox; and the Hopkinsville Hoppers with the Nashville Vols of the Southern Association.

Despite a soggy diamond, the Municipal Park grandstand overflowed with 8,961 fans as the Generals began the season on May 3 against the Hopkinsville Hoppers. Left-hander Dick Janasky, in

Top Row: Walkup, Melton, Pruitt, Stewart, Addison, Stephens, Valadez, Kreiger, Tilly. Bottom Row: Sventko, Ray, Martin, Hedges, Tomchak, Ross, Martindale.

WELCOME

The Jackson Baseball Association welcomes you to its game and sincerely appreciates your patronage.

The merchants who advertise on our fence or on this score card, of the citizens of this area. This ball park is an example of what can be accomplished when private enterprise, city government, and city merchants combine their efforts to promote a civic venture.

The merchants who advertise on our fence or on this score card, you people who attend the game, the Fair Association who made available the grounds, the City Commissioners who cooperated in the fullest, and all of the civic organizations in Jackson are entitled to the credit for baseball returning to Jackson.

It's Your Team!

JACKSON BASEBALL ASS'N Inc.

his second year of professional ball, took the hill for the Generals but ran into trouble in the eighth inning, loading the bases with two outs and a 3-3 tie. The Hopkinsville bench jockeys taunted his replacement, Clyde Barger, calling him "Old Sore Arm." The Milan, Tennessee native promptly fired three fastballs down the middle to strike out pinch hitter Pat Savro and end the inning. In their half of the eighth, the Generals countered by loading the bases and, with two outs, brought up their own pinch hitter, the left-hand-hitting Dominic Italiano. The Hoppers bench erupted again, calling him a "popcorn hitter." The St. Louis native responded by popping a single down the first base line that scored the go-ahead run and put Jackson in the lead, 4-3. The Hopkinsville dugout was silent in the ninth when Barger snubbed another potential Hopper rally and preserved the Generals' first victory. Light-hitting shortstop Leo Martindale, a Jackson native, hit a single and a double and drove in two runs in the game.

After losing their next two at Hopkinsville, the Generals started a habit of winning in double figures. They traveled to Cairo and swept their two-game series there by scores of 11-3 and 11-6, then came back home to beat Mayfield 13-7. But the Clothiers gave them a dose of their own medicine with an 18-9 defeat. Jackson quickly rebounded by winning their next two from Mayfield and Union City with 29 more runs. Their high-scoring offense landed them in second place, just one game behind first-place Hopkinsville, but they dropped 14 of their next 21 games to fall as far as fifth place by the first week of June.

On June 8, the Generals fell into sixth place with a record of 15-19. Three days later, they beat fourth-place Mayfield 11-4 with 15 hits, including a 3-for-5 debut by new second baseman Bearl Brooks. The Monette, Arkansas native hit .483 with eight RBIs and two stolen bases to contribute to their season-high nine-game winning streak. When it was over, Jackson was in third place and four games above .500. Dick Janasky shut out the last-place Cairo Dodgers on June 23, allowing only four hits while striking out 11. Their 5-0 victory tied them with the Owensboro Oilers for the league lead.

A major contributor to the Generals' June success was center fielder Maurice Partain. The lanky 20-year-old from Nashville, Tennessee had 22 stolen bases in the month (37 total) and at point had more thefts by himself than three Kitty League teams had. The stolen base was Partain's trademark in his two seasons with Jackson and made him one of the most popular members of the team. "Some reason or other, they always wanted me to steal every time I got on," he remembered.

Depending on who was on the mound, Partain wasn't shy about letting the opposing catcher know his intentions. "He would like to get up to the plate," teammate Dominic Italiano recalled, "and he would tell the catcher, 'If I get to first base,' he says, 'I'm going to run on the first pitch.' And he would. He liked to brag about [it] because he knew he could do it." "Yeah, I did that quite often," Partain admitted with a smile. "Because you didn't steal on him [the catcher] anyway." And he wasn't always satisfied with just one: The swift outfielder had at least 18 multi-steal games and stole three bases in a game twice during the season.

The addition of Harold "Hal" Seawright on June 24 gave the Generals the power hitter they sorely lacked. The 27-year-old veteran had already played five seasons in the minors, starting out with the Fulton Chicks in 1946. He spent the next three years with Greenville, Mississippi in the Class C Cotton States League, where he led the league in hitting at .326 with 108 RBIs in 1949. He was player-manager for his hometown Cairo Dodgers at the beginning of the 1950 season, but was blamed for the team's last-place standing despite leading the league in hitting. The Dodgers released him when a new skipper was signed.

THE 1950 GENERALS. LEFT TO RIGHT (TOP ROW): DOYLE PRUETT, BOB EVANS, MIKE CONOVAN, ROY WALKUP, ED KRIEGER, GABBY STEWART, LEE VALADEZ, MAURICE PARTAIN, DAVID ROSS. BOTTOM ROW: BEARL BROOKS, WALT MESTAN, LEN ADDISON, HAYDEN RAY, BILLY REED (BATBOY), DON STEVENS, DICK JANASKY, DOMINIC ITALIANO, LEO MARTINDALE.

Already at the four-player league limit for veterans on the team, the Generals placed Gabby Stewart on the inactive list for one game to accommodate Seawright's addition before releasing veteran third baseman Cecil Hubbard. Many in the league wondered how Jackson could have his reported $350-a-month salary on its roster and stay within the league limit of $2,600.

The investment was worth it as the short-legged, tobacco-chewing outfielder became a fan favorite in Jackson. Local sportswriter Jimmy Hamlin nicknamed him "Li'l Humphrey" for his short stature and less-than-stellar defense. With Seawright in left and fellow slugger Bob Samaras in right, Maury Partain was kept busy in center all season long. "They always told me, 'We'll get the fouls and you get the fairs,'" he recalled. Despite being a defensive liability in the field, he more than made up for it with his bat, hitting .317 with nine home runs and 38 RBIs in 49 games for the Generals. "You throw that ball a little high on him and he'd hit it out of the ballpark," Dominic Italiano remembered. "He had that much strength."

MAURICE PARTAIN AND HAL SEAWRIGHT

In his third game with Jackson on June 25, Seawright socked a thord-inning grand slam to give his new team the lead over the Mayfield Clothiers. His teammates contributed 10 more runs (seven in the sixth inning alone) to beat them 14-10 and give the team sole possession of first place. Starting pitcher Bob Evans allowed five runs on five hits before collapsing from a heat stroke in the fifth inning. He was relieved by Walt Mestan, who took the win. The Kentuckians protested the game, claiming that the Generals had exceeded the league limit with five veterans on the field. The protest was dropped when it was learned Stewart, though managing and coaching from third base box, was temporarily an inactive player.

Despite a temporary setback the next day (losing 15-0 to Mayfield and committing nine errors), the Generals stayed atop the league standings for over a week. Being in first place on July 4, Jackson won the privilege of hosting the Kitty League All-Star Game. Two days later, right-handed pitcher Bill Chambers, acquired with third baseman Emil Kirik in a four-player deal with the Union City Greyhounds, had a no-hitter in the works against the Madisonville Miners at Municipal Park. Leading 1-0, an infield hit in the sixth inning broke up the former University of Kentucky football player's no-hit bid. A double and a single followed, erasing his shutout and giving Madisonville a 2-1 victory. The defeat, coupled with Owensboro's 6-2 win over Hopkinsville, dropped the Generals from the league lead. After winning the second game of the doubleheader, they lost their next four to fall back into fifth place, three games behind the first-place Mayfield Clothiers.

Right-handers Dick Janasky and Walt Mestan emerged as the two leading hurlers on the pitching staff. Janasky led the team with a 3.38 ERA and was second in the league with 130 strikeouts while finishing with a record of 15-9. Mestan led the staff with his 16-5 mark and ended the season with 118 strikeouts and a 3.43 ERA. Bill Chambers gave the team a reliable third starter after he was acquired from Union City the first week of July and contributed a 5-5 record with 54 strikeouts in 12 games. Hard-throwing left-hander Tillman West "Mike" Conovan was third on the staff with nine victories and 107 strikeouts.

Now a second division club, Jackson hosted the All-Star Game at Municipal Park on July 11. Some 3,000 fans packed the Fairgrounds grandstand to see the contest. Bespectacled Dick Janasky started for the Generals, giving up three runs on three hits and a walk in the first four innings. Mike Conovan took over in the fifth, but allowed two more runs to score on six hits and a walk in his four innings of work. He was relieved by Jackson native David Ross in the ninth, who gave up only two hits, but the Generals dropped the Kitty League classic 5-3. It was Janasky's second consecutive loss in the All-Star Game, having dropped the 1949 contest while with the Clarksville Colts. Jackson collected 10 hits

Generals Fact
Jackson hosted the Kitty League All-Star Game four times—1937, 1940, 1941, and 1950.

The 1950 Generals pitching staff. Top row: Dick Janasky, Clyde Barger, Walt Mestan, Robert Evans. Bottow row: David Ross, Bill Chambers, Roy Walkup.

off four All-Star hurlers, while the league's best had 12. Gabby Stewart was the hitting star of the contest, going 4-for-5 with two doubles (the only extra base hits of the contest) and one RBI. Bearl Brooks, Maury Partain, and Hal Seawright each had two hits in five at-bats. Madisonville right fielder Joseph Krawezak led the All-Stars with his 3-for-5 performance.

During the season, Jackson had an opponent in the umpiring ranks in Robert Swisher. Their problems started when Swisher, while calling balls and strikes at Cairo, told the Generals' catcher that he would make sure pitcher Bill Chambers would be put out of the game and proceeded to call every pitch a ball until Gabby Stewart was forced to take him out. Dominic Italiano recalled another encounter with Swisher during an at-bat against a sidearm pitcher. The umpire called the first pitch inside a strike. "He threw three pitches like that and I almost had to back away and put my stomach in," he remembered. "Of course, after that third pitch, I really kind of griped about it...And he came up to

DICK JANASKY

me and kind of pushed me and challenged me to a fight." Gabby Stewart quickly intervened to prevent an altercation. The final straw came in the Generals' 17-2 loss to Madisonville on August 20. In the second inning, Swisher called a Madisonville runner safe at second. First baseman Italiano questioned the call and was promptly ejected by Swisher, who then challenged him to a fight after the game. Shortstop Lee Valadez intervened, asking the umpire if he "had a chip on his shoulder," which led to *his* ejection. Russell Rice, executive secretary for the club, demanded that league president Shelby Peace remove Swisher from the umpiring ranks for his "high-temper, unfairness, and general inefficiency." Although he was not fired immediately, Swisher did not return the following season.

The Generals regained their winning momentum after the All-Star Game, taking 13 of their next 17 games. Right-hander Walt Mestan topped off the team's five-game winning streak on July 29 with a three-hitter (his second in as many starts), shutting out the Union City Greyhounds 15-0. The victory put them in second place, 1½ games behind Mayfield, but only three percentage points ahead of the powerful Fulton Railroaders and seven ahead of the fourth-place Owensboro Oilers. The next day, both teams leapfrogged over Jackson with their loss to the Greyhounds and forced them into fourth place.

During the final weeks of the season, Jackson fans counted down Maury Partain's pursuit of the Kitty League single-season stolen base record. The record was 84 held by Don Hazelton, who set the mark with Owensboro the previous season. Going into August, Partain had 56 and needed 27 more to tie it. He stole three against the Hopkinsville Hoppers on August 27 to give him 81 with only two games left in the season. Rain the next day forced a season-ending doubleheader at Hopkinsville on August 29. In the first game, Partain reached base on every at-bat but did not have a steal. He went all-out to tie the record in the second inning of the second game, stealing second, then third, and finally sprinting home to tie it. The play was close, but the umpire called him out. Partain had three more at-bats in the game, but failed to reach base and ended the season just one steal shy of tying the record.

Generals Fact
Maurice Partain came within one stolen base of tying the Kitty League record in a season. Don Hazelton of the Owensboro Oilers had set the record of 84 in 1949.

Though the Generals were still within striking distance of first-place Mayfield, it became more important for them to stay in the first division to gain a berth in the postseason Shaughnessy playoffs. Jackson, Fulton, and Owensboro stayed neck-and-neck throughout the last month of the season with second place changing hands regularly. But in the last week, the General lost four straight to the Oilers and slid from a second-place tie with Fulton into fifth, three percentage points behind the Madisonville Miners with four games left in the season. They rebounded the next day with a victory over Owensboro to jump into third place, forcing the Oilers temporarily into the second division.

The Generals began a four-game series with Hopkinsville on August 26, the first two being played at home. The players were exhausted: After leaving Owensboro at about midnight, the team bus broke down and it took twelve hours to reach Jackson. Starter Roy Walkup was shaky, giving up six runs in the first three innings to put his team in a 6-5 deficit through the first seven. Jackson mounted a comeback in the eighth, scoring five runs, one of them on a steal of home by Maury Partain. Reliever Clyde Barger took over for Walkup in the top of the ninth, protecting a 10-6 lead, but the Hoppers got four runs off him to tie the score and send the game into extra innings. Madisonville had already won their game, so a Jackson loss would further cement them in the second division and out of the playoffs. Hal Seawright led off in the bottom of the eleventh with the score still tied. On the first pitch delivered by Hoppers manager Joe DeMasi, Seawright blasted it over the left field fence to give the Generals the 11-10 victory. They ended the season on August 29, winning both games of a doubleheader at Hopkinsville to finish in third place at 68-52, six games behind the league champion Mayfield Clothiers.

The Generals faced the second-place Fulton Railroaders in the semifinals of the Shaughnessy playoffs. The best-of-five series began at Fulton on August 30 with Walt Mestan facing 15-game winner Charles Tate. The Generals gave their ace a four-run lead in the first inning, but the young right-hander's wildness forced his early exit after only an inning and two-thirds. He

Andy Sventko, Don Stevens, Doyle Pruett, and Len Addison pose behind the Generals team bus in 1950.

walked five, hit a batter, and yielded four hits to give the Kentuckians a 5-4 lead. Jackson pushed two more runs across in the fifth and sixth and led 6-5 before the Railroaders tied it up in the bottom of the ninth. Fulton's big first baseman Ned Waldrop capped a 4-for-6 performance with a grand slam off Clyde Barger in the twelfth to give his team the first game, 10-6.

Rain forced the second game to be postponed until September 1, when another extra inning affair went in Fulton's favor. Bill Chambers allowed seven hits, striking out nine and walking only two, but Fulton's Harley Grossman was equally effective, holding the Generals to eight hits while fanning eight and walking none. Former Generals were the deciding factors in the game: Catcher Len Addison's RBI single drove in the tying run in the bottom of the ninth and third baseman Cecil Hubbard scored the winning run in the tenth after being hit by a pitch to give the Railroaders a 3-2 victory and a two-game lead in the series.

The series went to Municipal Park the next evening, but rain once again forced its postponement. Jackson won their first game on

A RARE PHOTO OF THE GENERALS ROAD UNIFORM AS WORN BY WALT MESTAN IN HIS UNION CITY HOTEL ROOM.

September 3 behind the pitching of Dick Janasky, who held Fulton scoreless through the first seven innings to win 5-1. Extra innings were needed once again to decide the fourth game. With the score tied 3-3 in the sixth, Ned Waldrop hit his second home run of the series to give his team a one-run lead. It was short-lived, however, as Generals right fielder Bob Samaras answered with his second round-tripper in the eighth to knot it up again. With the winning run on third for the third consecutive frame, Jackson finally drove it in on Bearl Brooks' single in the twelfth to win 5-4 and tie the series at two games apiece.

The fifth and deciding game on September 5 saw a pitching rematch of the second game with the same result. right-hander Bill Chambers allowed nine singles and helped his own cause, hitting a triple and scoring a run in the fifth inning. Fulton starter Harley Grossman yielded only seven hits, one being an RBI double by Hal Seawright that gave Jackson the initial lead. The Generals led 2-1 through the first six innings, but the Railroaders tied it in the seventh and won it on a hit-and-run in the ninth, 3-2, with former General Cecil Hubbard scored the winning tally. Gabby Stewart tried to spark a ninth inning rally with a leadoff single, but Bob Samaras, Dominic Italiano, and Emil Kirik each grounded out to end the game. Fulton advanced to the finals against Mayfield, but the series was canceled due to excessive rainouts.

1950 Kitty League Standings

Team	W	L	PCT	GB
Mayfield Clothiers	73	45	.619	—
Fulton Railroaders	69	50	.580	4.5
Jackson Generals	68	52	.567	6
Owensboro Oilers	64	51	.557	7.5
Madisonville Miners	63	51	.553	8
Hopkinsville Hoppers	60	60	.500	14
Union City Greyhounds	43	72	.374	28.5
Cairo Dodgers	26	85	.234	43.5

Shaughnessy playoffs—Fulton beat Jackson 3 games to 2 and Mayfield beat Owensboro 3 games to 2.

Finals—Mayfield led against Fulton 1 game to none when the series was cancelled due to constant rainouts.

1951

Finish	Record	Pct.	GB
Fifth	(59-61)	.492	14.5

Manager	Record	Pct.
Glen (Gabby) Stewart	(59-61)	.492

Attendance	Lg Rank
24,961	Sixth

Former Major Leaguers
Glen (Gabby) Stewart

Starting Lineup
C	Glen (Gabby) Stewart	.329 BA
1B	Victor (Vic) Pierson	.244 BA
2B	Bearl Brooks	.273 BA
3B	Clyde Barger	.238 BA
SS	Lee Valadez	.285 BA
LF	Harold (Hal) Seawright	.337 BA
CF	Maurice Partain	.286 BA
RF	Fred Henry	.235 BA

Pitching Staff
RH	Bill Chambers	(16-11)
RH	Walt Mestan	(14-6)
LH	James Kluck	(10-8)
	Arthur (Art) Chivers	(8-6)
LH	Richard (Dick) Janasky	(5-6)

Top 10 Batters and Top 5 Pitchers

Batter	BA	G	AB	R	H	2B	3B	HR	RBI	SB
Hal Seawright	.337	118	478	90	161	31	4	16	122	9
Gabby Stewart	.329	117	401	67	132	33	8	2	96	8
Maurice Partain	.286	75	315	79	90	14	4	1	40	35
Lee Valadez	.285	112	425	107	121	11	7	1	61	25
Bearl Brooks	.273	112	469	102	128	11	6	1	55	44
Roy Del Rio	.257	30	113	11	29	3	2	0	28	5
Victor Pierson*	.244	97	324	49	79	21	6	0	38	2
Clyde Barger	.238	115	411	53	98	5	4	0	64	7
Fred Henry	.235	28	98	12	23	3	2	1	18	3
Scott Irwin*	.228	116	412	63	94	19	6	0	54	13

Pitcher	ERA	G	IP	W	L	CG	ER	Sh	BB	SO
Bill Chambers	2.39	29	222	16	11	24	59	0	119	158
Walt Mestan	2.86	21	170	14	6	15	54	1	87	157
Dick Janasky	3.01	12	87	5	6	7	29	1	21	38
Jim Kluck	—	19	145	10	8	13	—	2	49	50

* Also with the Paducah Chiefs

The 1951 Generals retained their veteran nucleus as well as the younger players who had gained experience during the previous season. The Kitty League cut team rosters from 17 to 15 players, but encouraged the addition of more veterans with six allowed per club and seven class players with previous professional experience, leaving room for only two rookies. Cairo lost its franchise to Paducah over the winter and the league salary cap was set at $2,300 a month.

To bolster attendance for the upcoming season, the Jackson Baseball Association encouraged local youngsters to join the "Junior Generals." For a membership fee of $1.50, young fans up to 12 years old received admission to 16 regular season home games, a membership card, and a "Junior General" baseball cap. Adults were offered a book of 20 grandstand tickets for $10.

The Generals started the season at home in front of 6,577 fans on May 6 against the Union City Greyhounds. With the bases loaded in the first inning, rookie third baseman Roy Del Rio drove a pitch to right center field that quickly clear them, but robbed himself of a sure triple after stumbling at first base and was held to a three-run single. Bill Chambers limited the Greyhounds to five singles for the 8-1 victory. The Huntingdon, West Virginia native reeled off five consecutive wins as Jackson won 11 of their first 17 games to climb into second place, just 1½ games behind the first-place Fulton Railroaders.

After two losses to the Paducah Chiefs, the Generals hosted Fulton for a three-game series in late May with the chance to overtake the league leaders. But the Railroaders' effective pitching and the Generals' lack of it stifled their takeover attempt and the visitors easily swept the series. In two of the three games, Jackson was forced to use at least three pitchers to counter Fulton's potent offense, allowing 30 hits in both contests. Chambers lost his first game of the season despite giving up only eight hits as Fulton ace Walt Bryja (who went on to win 24 games during the season) tossed a four-hitter to take the final game 5-2. Another loss to Mayfield on May 29 dropped them into fifth place and 5½ games out of first.

Toward the end of May, the Generals added Brooklyn Dodgers farmhand Raymond Earl "Tobe" Bailey Jr. to their pitching staff. The Jackson native asked the Dodgers organization to send him to his hometown team rather than their Class D Hazard, Kentucky farm club. He spent the rest of the month with them primarily as a reliever with a 1-2 record.

Jackson began the month of June winning only two of their first seven

WALT MESTAN

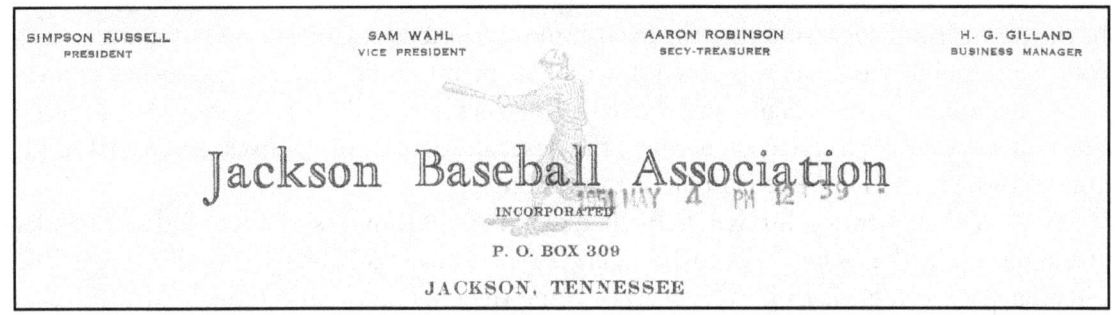

THE JACKSON BASEBALL ASSOCIATION LETTERHEAD FOR THE 1951 SEASON

games. Then they caught fire, taking 16 of their remaining 21 to put them back in second place and only 1½ games behind Fulton. Their winning streak started with Walt Mestan's 3-0 shutout against Union City, the first of the season for the Generals. The Chicago right-hander limited the Greyhounds to three hits but caused some anxious moments by loading the bases with two outs in the eighth inning. A force out squeezed him out of the predicament. Mestan, Chambers, and newly-acquired left-hander Jim Kluck each won four games with another recent addition, former Hopkinsville southpaw Mel Weiser, contributing two.

Eighteen-year-old Jim Kluck had been released by the Owensboro Oilers, who felt that he wasn't a winning pitcher. The Stevens Point, Wisconsin native proved them wrong, at least initially, tossing a four-hitter over 11 innings against Paducah in his debut on June 16. Four days later he had a no-hitter going into the ninth at Fulton until shortstop Billy Joe Forrest spoiled it with a leadoff single. He settled for a one-hitter and a 2-0 shutout.

During their winning streak, the never-say-die Generals won 11 of their 16 victories by three runs or less, seven by dramatic late-inning rallies. On June 14 Walt Mestan and Mayfield pitcher Angie Orlando dueled into extra innings with the Jackson right-hander yielding only four hits. Right fielder Fred AuBuchon singled home the winning run in the thirteenth and put the Generals only two percentage points behind the fourth-place Mayfield Clothiers. Two more victories temporarily boosted them into third, but they lost their position to the Union City Greyhounds three days later.

Kluck's third consecutive win, a 4-3 victory at Madisonville, put Jackson back in second place as they prepared for another head-to-head series at Municipal Park with the league-leading Fulton Railroaders on June 27. They took the first two games by comfortable margins, 7-3 and 9-2, to come within 1½ games of first place, but gave the Railroaders three unearned runs to lose the final game 4-3.

Despite their on-the-field success, the club was struggling financially and there were indications that the principal owners and stockholders of the Jackson Baseball Association were ready to sell. The Generals had a large showing on Opening Day (though it was 2,384 less than the previous season), but attendance declined considerably the remainder of the season as home games typically attracted less than 200 fans. The team finished the season sixth in the eight-team circuit in overall attendance at 24,961, a decrease of 5,117 from the previous year. It is interesting to note that the Union City Greyhounds were third with 33,652 despite fielding a sixth-place club.

The Association hoped that local ownership would purchase the franchise and keep baseball in Jackson, although a Bowling Green, Kentucky group had already expressed interest in the team. It was suggested that the local Junior Chamber of Commerce buy the club as a civic venture, but the effort was voted down by its membership. Several late-season promotions, including Shriners' Night and the Miss Jackson General Beauty Contest, helped bring more fans to the ballpark and encouraged the Baseball Association to invest additional funds and keep the franchise the remainder of the season.

After Mel Weiser and Jim Kluck pitched dual five-hit shutouts in a July 2 doubleheader at Hopkinsville, the Generals lost 12 of their next 16 games to fall back into fifth place. The pitching staff struggled, with Walt Mestan being the only consistent winner. Arm soreness put staff ace Bill Chambers on the shelf for two weeks. After winning his first five games with the team, Kluck lost his next seven and finished the season at 9-9 for Jackson (12-13 overall). Prodigal son Dick Janasky returned to the fold after leaving two months earlier for a higher salary in a Minnesota semi-pro league, but was winless in his first four starts back.

BILL CHAMBERS

Mestan snapped the club's five-game losing skid on July 11 with a near no-hitter (his third of the season) against fourth-place Owensboro. But just like his three previous attempts, the unlucky hit came in the seventh inning. After a walk to the first batter, Oilers left fielder J.T. Jaynes drove a pitch down the right field line. When outfielder Dominic Italiano tried to field the ball on one hop, but it took a bad bounce and got past him, rolling to the fence and allowing the runner on first to score. It was Owenboro's only run, however, as Mestan finished with a one-hitter and a 10-1 victory.

Walt Mestan gave the Generals a dependable and effective starter to complement Bill Chambers, though it looked early on like the team would be without his services for the season. During the winter, the Chicago native stayed in Jackson and started his own plastering business, making enough money that he no longer needed to play baseball. But Aaron Robinson, one of the team owners, persuaded him to return and pitch exclusively at home and a few road games close by. Mestan had another good season, finishing second behind Chambers in wins (14) and strikeouts (156) with a 2.68 ERA. His strikeout total was third-best in the Kitty League and his ERA seventh-best.

Chambers led the Generals' pitching staff with 16 victories, finishing second in the league with 157 strikeouts and leading the circuit with 24 complete games. After the season was over, the Jackson High School teacher and assistant football coach was drafted by the

Class B Portsmouth, Virginia Cubs of the Piedmont League, where he twirled a no-hitter in 1952.

The team offense was slowed considerably when leading base stealer Maurice Partain broke his leg while sliding into second base at Mayfield on July 19. At the time, the lanky center fielder had 35 stolen bases en route to a team goal of 200 swipes during the season. The injury not only ended his season but his career as well. The Generals finished well below their goal with only 146, though it was still enough to lead the league. Second baseman Bearl Brooks surpassed Partain to led the team with 44 stolen bases.

Jackson had three representatives in the Kitty League All-Star Game held at Fulton's Fairfield Park on July 24. Left fielder Hal Seawright led the All-Stars with a perfect 5-for-5 performance, slugging a home run, two doubles, and driving in four runs in their 6-2 victory over the Railroaders. right-hander Bill Chambers pitched two innings of scoreless relief, allowing only two hits and striking out two. Versatile Clyde Barger played third base but was hitless in two at-bats.

The Generals took advantage of the seventh-place Madisonville Miners in a four-game weekend series at Municipal Park to jump back into the first division. The first game saw pitcher Dick Janasky start out as the home plate umpire and end as the closer on the mound. A torrential downpour on the other end of town kept the umpires from being on time for the July 29 contest, so the two managers agreed on one player from each team officiating until the regular arbiters showed up. Janasky, having already pitched two days earlier, was chosen to call the balls and strikes from behind the plate while Miners hurler Ed Santa worked the bases. The arrangement lasted only an inning before the regular umpires replaced them and Janasky returned to the bench, his night presumably over. But in the ninth, with the bases loaded, only one out, and Jackson clinging to a four-run lead, Gabby Stewart lifted starter Bill Chambers and called him in. The bespectacled right-hander induced the next batter to pop up to left field and ended the threat with a strikeout to preserve the 6-2 victory.

Rookie right-hander Howard Ralph limited Madisonville to seven hits in the first game of the Saturday doubleheader, holding them scoreless in all but one inning to win 6-3. The second game, played under the lights, was a free-for-all for the home team. Led by Hal Seawright and Clyde Barger, the Jackson offense pounded three Miners hurlers (including manager Burl Storie) for 22 hits. Both hitters had five hits in six at-bats, with Seawright belting a home run and driving in seven runs, tying him for the most RBIs by a Generals player in one game. (Mel Merkel set the mark on September 12, 1941) Walt Mestan took full advantage of the 17-run cushion his teammates gave him, stifling the Madisonville offense with 12 strikeouts while allowing only eight hits to win 19-2. The twin victories elevated the Generals into a third-place tie with the Mayfield Clothiers.

The team honored utility player Clyde Barger for his versatility the past two seasons with a "night" in his honor on July 29. Local fans showered the Milan, Tennessee cotton farmer with numerous gifts, including a shoebox filled with dollar bills and loose change. He started at third base and contributed two hits, including a triple, two RBIs, and a run scored, to

> **Generals Fact**
> On July 29, Generals pitcher Dick Janasky started the game as an emergency home-plate umpire and ended it as a reliever, preserving a 6-2 win against the Madisonville Miners.

Clyde Barger beside the Generals' dugout

help his team win the fourth and final game of the series, 8-1, and give the Generals sole possession of third place.

Jackson's offensive attack was powered for the second straight season by left fielder Hal Seawright and catcher-manager Gabby Stewart. The hard-hitting Seawright was the club's lone home run threat, accounting for all but seven of the Generals' round-trippers in 1951. He led the Kitty League in most offensive categories, including hits (161), total bases (248), RBIs (122), and batting average (.337), while muscling 16 long balls out of league ballparks, only two behind home run champion Joseph Duhem of Mayfield. Seawright spent the next two seasons fighting in the Korean War before ending his professional career under former teammate Bearl Brooks at Hopkinsville in 1954. Gabby Stewart continued to be one of the best defensive catchers in the league as well as a productive hitter, batting .329 and leading his team with 33 doubles and eight triples while driving in 96 runs.

The Generals' successful climb back into the first division during the eventful Madisonville series disappeared going into the last month of the season. They held fourth place for the first week of August but dropped two out of three at home to the Paducah Chiefs to fall back into the second division. There was a brief one-game return to third place (a tie with Union City) after an August 11 victory at Madisonville, but they lost their next five straight to fall back into fifth, 8½ games behind league-leading Owensboro. Three of them came against the Miners, who got even with the Generals by taking two one-run games and humiliating them with a six-hit, 19-0 defeat. They were handed another one-sided loss by the third-place Mayfield Clothiers the next day, 27-10. The Generals had four non-pitchers taking turns on the mound: Hal Seawright, Vic Pierson, Fred Henry, and Dick Thomas.

Walt Mestan took his fourth no-hitter of the season into the seventh inning on August 10, only to watch a one-out double erase it. The Chicago right-hander struck out 11 Paducah batters and held them to four hits. Two hits mixed with two walks and an infield error, however, to give the Chiefs a four-run seventh and a 5-2 victory. It was only his second loss of the season at Municipal Park, having won 11 straight decisions there.

A week later, Mestan was locked in a pitcher's duel at home against Mayfield right-hander Bert Gibbs. The game was scoreless until the seventh when the Clothiers tagged the Jackson hurler for three runs on five hits. In the Generals' half, cleanup hitter Hal Seawright disputed a called strike from home plate umpire Barney Deary too strongly and was thrown out of the game. The unpopular ousting set the stage for the ninth inning when Mestan, with two outs and a runner on third trying to score, took the cutoff throw and thought he had tagged him out at the plate. But Dreary called the runner safe and immediately received an earful from the irate pitcher. The arbiter heard enough and tossed him from the game, prompting several fans to rush onto the field and halt the game for a short time. After the Generals' 6-1 loss, several Jackson policemen had to escort the embattled umpire from the field for his own safety.

After their 10-4 loss to Owensboro in the first game of an August 22 doubleheader, Jackson dropped below .500 for the first time since June. The second game featured yet another near no-hitter, this time by Jackson native David Ross, who gave up a home run in the sixth inning that barely made it inside the foul pole. Despite the team's second division finish, a capacity crowd of more than 4,000 packed the Municipal Park grandstand to see the Generals end their season on a winning note, beating the Paducah Chiefs 9-5. Overall, they finished in fifth place, 14½ games behind the champion Fulton Railroaders (who took over the league lead during the last weekend of the season), with a record of 59-61.

1951 Kitty League Standings

Team	W	L	Pct.	GB
Fulton Railroaders	73	46	.613	—
Owensboro Oilers	71	48	.597	2
Mayfield Clothiers	66	53	.555	7
Paducah Chiefs*	64	55	.538	9
Jackson Generals	**59**	**61**	**.492**	**14.5**
Union City Greyhounds	57	63	.475	16.5
Madisonville Miners	46	73	.387	27
Hopkinsville Hoppers	41	78	.345	32

*Cairo franchise awarded to Paducah, Kentucky in the off-season

Shaughnessy playoffs—Fulton beat Paducah 3 games to 2. Owensboro beat Mayfield 3 games to 1.

Finals—Fulton beat Owensboro 4 games to none

1952

Finish	Record	Pct.	GB
Seventh	(48-71)	.403	34

Managers	Record	Pct.
Vince Pankovits	(13-14)	.482
Dominic Italiano	(27-45)	.375
George (Mickey) O'Neil	(8-12)	.400

Attendance	Lg Rank
27,647	Seventh

Former Major Leaguers
Mickey O'Neil

Starting Lineup
C	Dominic Italiano	.274 BA
1B	Victor (Vic) Pierson	.209 BA
2B	Bearl Brooks	.237 BA
3B	Joseph (Joe) Thomas	.280 BA
SS	Robert (Bob) Grose	.249 BA
LF	Lonnie Eastham	.272 BA
CF	Lee Valadez	.240 BA
RF	Vito Valenzano	.237 BA

Pitching Staff
LH	Tillman (Mike) Conovan	(20-12)
RH	Howard Ralph	(9-14)
RH	Cliff Walling	(6-7)
RH	Robert (Bob) Brewer	(2-13)

Top 10 Batters and Top 5 Pitchers

Batter	BA	G	AB	R	H	2B	3B	HR	RBI	SB
Howard Bierman	.318	44	157	23	50	7	3	0	21	6
Joseph Thomas	.280	60	189	41	53	7	2	1	8	13
Dominic Italiano	.274	87	285	74	78	18	1	8	76	12
Lonnie Eastham*	.272	94	375	54	102	9	3	3	46	12
Robert Grose	.249	117	442	81	110	10	4	0	44	14
Lee Valadez	.240	100	362	49	87	8	4	1	48	9
Vito Valenzano	.237	90	266	30	63	8	3	0	30	7
Bearl Brooks	.237	55	232	42	55	3	2	1	27	14
Robert Friskel	.236	43	144	22	34	2	1	0	11	4
Vincent Pierson	.209	76	234	28	49	8	1	2	39	5

Pitcher	ERA	G	IP	W	L	CG	ER	Sh	BB	SO
Mike Conovan	3.46	47	281	20	12	24	108	2	224	345
Bob Brewer	3.63	20	109	2	13	4	44	2	65	75
Joe May	4.26	25	112	5	10	4	53	1	62	51
Cliff Walling	5.01	31	140	6	7	8	78	0	81	55
Howard Ralph	5.54	36	195	9	14	12	78	0	81	55

* Also with the Mayfield Clothiers

THE 1952 SEASON

The Jackson Baseball Association, having suffered heavy financial losses and low attendance with two high-priced veteran clubs, built the 1952 Generals on a foundation of untested rookies and limited service players, with Dominic Italiano, Lee Valadez, Bearl Brooks, Vic Pierson, and Mike Conovan the only returning veterans. Vince Pankovits of Long Island, New York was signed as the new player-manager, replacing the popular Gabby Stewart. He had played several seasons in the Boston Braves' farm system before managing the Pennington Gap, West Virginia club of the Mountain States League in 1951.

The Generals dropped their first game of the season on May 4 in a 16-8 loss at Union City. Rookie right-hander Howard Ralph gave up nine runs on five hits and seven walks in almost five innings. He was replaced by Leo Martindale, who took the loss after allowing six runs himself in his only inning of work. They returned to Jackson for their home opener the next evening, but were set down on right-hander Joe May's three-hit, 4-0 shutout. An eight-run second-inning rally against the Greyhounds on May 6 gave the Generals their first victory, 11-5.

Jackson stayed in the first division during the first two weeks of the season, then fell into fifth place with a record of 13-14 by the end of the month. As a result, Pankovits was released as player-manager on May 30. Although the move was attributed to the team's record and his below-.200 hitting, the disposed manager believed it was his treatment of Mexican-American veteran Lee Valadez that led to his release. "I was there to more or less train ballplayers, not for individual records," Pankovits recalled. "That was secondary. He didn't play as much as he thought he needed to play." Local sportswriter Jimmy Hamlin hinted that some players thought Gabby Stewart had been a better player-manager. Another reason was his involvement in several heated arguments with league umpires and having already been thrown out of four games in less than four weeks.

> **Generals Fact**
> Vince Pankovits, manager of the 1952 Generals, is the father of Jim Pankovits, manager of the Generals in 2011 and 2012.

Pankovits was replaced by veteran catcher-first baseman Dominic Italiano, who was in his third season with Jackson. The son of Italian immigrants, Dominic was born in St. Louis and grew up in the Italian section known as The Hill. Among the neighborhood kids he played sandlot ball with were Joe Garagiola and Lawrence "Yogi" Berra. He and Yogi played on the Stockham American Legion Post team together, with Italiano catching and Berra in the outfield. While Garagiola signed with the Cardinals and Berra with the Yankees, "Dom" started his professional career with the St. Louis Browns and was assigned to the Jackson, Mississippi club of the Class C Cotton States League in 1947. After his release, he played two years at Helena, Arkansas before being sold to the Generals in 1950. With manager Gabby Stewart handling the catching duties, he played first base and served as the reserve backstop. His hustling style made him popular with the local fans.

Italiano made his managerial debut on May 31 a winning one by hitting a three-run home run over the right field fence at Mayfield to give his club a 5-1 victory. Despite a weak offense, weaker pitching staff, and rumors of the teams' possible move to Dyersburg, the Generals won 10 of their first 15 games under their new skipper to climb into third place and back into the first division with a 23-19 record, just two percentage points out of second place and six games behind the league-leading Fulton Lookouts. Italiano hit .375 during the two-week span

Dominic Italiano

Hiram Hopper

with four homers and 23 RBIs. left-hander Mike Conovan, having missed the previous season with a sore arm, tossed a two-hitter and fanned 12 Clothiers on May 2, but was upstaged two days later by rookie right-hander Cliff Walling's one-hitter against Hopkinsville that pushed Jackson above .500. The no-hit bid was lost in the opening frame when former General Leon AuBuchon singled and his brother Fred (also an ex-General) scored an unearned run to rob him of a shutout.

As the Generals were climbing into the first division, it was announced that the club had been sold to a group of Dyersburg businessmen, who reportedly raised $30,000 to finance it. Initial plans were made for the transfer to take place on June 15 with the team playing at Burnham Field in Dyersburg. But the Baseball Association, preferring that the team stay in Jackson, instead sold it to local restaurant owner Hiram Hopper the next day. The Dyersburg group protested, claiming that they had a verbal agreement with Generals business manager Russell Rice and appealed in vain to Kitty League president Shelby Peace and National Association of Professional Baseball president George Trautman. Rice did not have the authority to sell the club, Peace stated, but needed the approval of the board of directors. Unable to get the franchise, they claimed that every Kitty League team (including Jackson) was violating the monthly salary limit and blasted Peace, vowing never to pursue another franchise "so long as Shelby Peace is president of the league."

Despite the threat of a legal injunction, Hopper officially took over the franchise on June 16, promising to help Italiano improve his roster as the manager saw fit. "If he wants a kangaroo to patrol the outfield," he joked, "I'll send to Australia and get him the biggest one I can find." Owning the Generals was a perfect fit for Hopper as his downtown restaurant, Hiram's at 211 East Main Street, was already a favorite hangout for many of the home and visiting players. "He was the type of man that cared about Jackson and they were going to lose the franchise," nephew Jim Bailey recalled. "I remember how mad Aunt Rachel got at him. But they didn't get a divorce."

Hopper made several initiatives to attract fans back to Municipal Park. The grandstand was cleaned inside and out, with accumulated garbage swept from the bleachers and soap and water applied to the outside of the building. Fans complained that it was too out-of-the-way, so the Jackson Transportation Company began running buses from the court square to the ballpark and back and Hub City Taxi Company had cars waiting for them after each game. The improvements resulted in larger crowds, at least until the team fell out of contention.

The Generals' winning outburst overshadowed the fact that the team was still last in the league in hitting and, except for Conovan and Walling, had an ineffective pitching staff. The lack of pitching depth forced Italiano to use them as relievers when not starting. It was a practice he was forced to use on several occasions and weakened his already overworked staff.

Jackson dropped four out of five to league-leading Fulton in mid June (including a 23-6 onslaught on June 15) and won only three more games the rest of the month, sliding back in fifth place. The team lost its most potent bat when Dominic Italiano went down, first with a sprained ankle in late June and then a broken finger in early July that sidelined him for over a month.

Without their hard-hitting manager in the lineup, the Generals descended even further into the second division. They had a horrible July, going 10-21 and hitting rock bottom on July 24 when they fell into last place after losing eight straight games, four of them to league-leading Fulton. Among the few highlights were Jackson's 17-8 victory over Hopkinsville on July 6 and Mike Conovan's two-hit shutout nine days later at Union City (despite giving up 12 walks). Except for brief one-game respites, the Generals were sole occupants in the league cellar the last five weeks of the season, threatening to become the only Generals team ever to finish in last place.

One of the team's losses was at Mayfield on July 8 against right-hander Mickey Stubblefield, who was the first African American to play in the Kitty League. He had played two years for the Kansas City Monarchs in the Negro American League, where he learned from Satchel Paige and even earned the nickname "Little Satchel." Stubblefield was set to pitch at Municipal Park on August 6, but rain postponed the game until the next day and he did not play. He finished the season at 7-6 with 70 strikeouts and a 3.72 ERA in 15 games.

One of the few bright spots of the 1952 season was the performance of veteran Mike Conovan, who was the team's most reliable and effective hurler. Despite recovering from a sore arm that forced him to miss the previous season, the hard-throwing left-hander never shied away from extra work, whether it was relieving or pitching both ends of a doubleheader. Conovan loved to show off his arm strength, once taking a water-soaked baseball to home plate and hurling it up and over the left field fence some 340 feet away (much to the horror of manager Dominic Italiano). "I can throw a new ball over the center field wall (a distance of 375 feet)," he boasted, "and I will when my arm gets good and rested."

Conovan and infielder Lee Valadez were selected as Jackson's representatives to the Kitty League All-Star team and played the first-place

MIKE CONOVAN

Fulton Lookouts at Fairfield Park on July 17. After giving up two runs on four walks and a hit to start the contest, Conovan settled down to shut them out in his new two innings pitched, but he was tagged with the 4-2 loss. Valadez made his first All-Star appearance in the third inning at third base, but went hitless in two at-bats.

With only three weeks left in a disappointing season, team owner Hiram Hopper brought back former Generals skipper Mickey O'Neil to lead the club the rest of the year. Italiano graciously offered him his assistance and hustling play, quickly winning the admiration of the new manager. "He is made out of the right kind of stuff," O'Neil remarked. "He is a perfect example of the boy I want to play for me." Casting a positive light on his dreadful club, O'Neil rationalized: "I can learn more about the ballclub when it loses than when it wins. I can see the mistakes better when we lose." The former major leaguer certainly got an eyeful as the Generals continued their downward spiral under his tenure.

As the season drew to a close, the only thing that brought the fans to Municipal Park was the pitching of Mike Conovan, who was chasing not only 20 wins but over 300 strikeouts. On August 27 the left-hander won his nineteenth game in a relief appearance against Union City and with six strikeouts broke Ellis Kinder's club record of 307 set in 1940. He also became only the third Kitty League pitcher ever to collect over 300 strikeouts in a season. In a losing effort against Owensboro two days later, the 25-year-old Medon, Tennessee native struck out 21 batters in 12 innings, the most by a Generals hurler since Orlin Collier fanned 22 in 1937. His twentieth victory came the next evening at home with a 9-8 win over Owensboro. Conovan ended the season with 345 strikeouts and 224 walks and a record of 20-12.

Generals Fact
Mike Conovan won 20 games for the seventh-place Generals and set a new club record with 345 strikeouts, breaking Ellis Kinder's mark of 307.

It looked like Conovan would achieve the rarity of winning 20 games for a last-place club. But the Generals spent the last month of the season trying to claw their way out of the cellar as Hopkinsville and Mayfield teetered on the brink of falling in themselves. They went into the last game of the season on September 1 still in last place, but with a glimmer of hope that a victory against Paducah and a Mayfield defeat would save Jackson the humiliation of a last-place finish. Right-hander Howard Ralph held Paducah to five hits as his teammates got 10 off Chiefs' pitching to win 8-4 and finish only one percentage point ahead of Mayfield, who with a season-ending loss dropped into the cellar. The Generals finished in seventh place with a record of 48-71, a staggering 34 games behind the league champion Fulton Lookouts.

1952 Kitty League Standings

Fulton Lookouts	82	37	.689	—
Paducah Chiefs	67	53	.558	15.5
Madiosnville Miners	65	55	.542	17.5
Union City Greyhounds	63	56	.529	19
Owensboro Oilers	58	65	.458	27.5
Hopkinsville Hoppers	50	70	.417	32.5
Jackson Generals	48	71	.403	34
Mayfield Clothiers	47	70	.402	34

Shaughnessy playoffs—Union City beat Fulton 3 games to 2. Madisonville beat Paducah 3 games to 1.

Finals—Madisonville beat Union City 3 games to 1

1953

Finish	Record	Pct.	GB
Sixth	(58-62)	.483	12

Manager	Record	Pct.
George (Mickey) O'Neil	(58-62)	.483

Attendance	Lg Rank
17,601	Eighth

Starting Lineup

C	Dominic Italiano	.226 BA, 41 RBIs
1B	Charles (Chick) Re	.259 BA, All-Star
2B	John Scercy	.231 BA, 14 HR
3B	Richard (Dick) Wehman	.283 BA, 82 RBIs
SS	Edward (Eddie) Miller	.272 BA, 21 SB
LF	Eugene (Gene) Bennett	.291 BA, 22 2B
CF	Jerry Elder	.297 BA, 13 SB
RF	Vincent (Vince) Monaco	.316 BA, 71 RBIs

Pitching Staff

LH	Ray D'Agrosa	(14-7)
RH	Howard Whitson	(13-12)
RH	Earl Gearhardt	(10-13)
RH	Carroll Drostie	(9-9)
RH	Ivan Mills	(7-12)

Top 10 Batters and Top 5 Pitchers

Batter	BA	G	AB	R	H	2B	3B	HR	RBI	SB
Vince Monaco	.316	96	361	52	114	15	7	10	71	8
Richard Gilliam	.304	25	102	25	31	1	3	1	16	3
Jerry Elder	.297	47	182	28	54	9	5	1	15	13
Gene Bennett	.291	91	371	60	108	22	8	4	83	23
Dick Wehman	.283	83	322	68	91	18	7	9	82	15
Ray D'Agrosa	.280	72	157	30	44	8	3	1	22	6
Eddie Miller	.272	112	441	81	120	19	4	1	51	21
Chick Re	.259	94	352	81	91	16	13	7	59	6
Bill Newkirk	.257	45	171	34	44	6	5	1	12	14
John Scercy	.231	95	329	67	76	21	6	14	67	15

Pitcher	ERA	G	IP	W	L	CG	ER	Sh	BB	SO
Howard Whitson	3.72	33	191	13	12	13	79	2	52	77
Ray D'Agrosa	4.31	28	169	14	7	13	81	0	95	158
Earl Gearhardt	5.44	32	184	10	13	13	111	0	69	113
Ivan Mills	5.69	28	155	7	12	9	98	1	85	129
Carroll Drostie	5.84	28	151	9	9	12	98	0	94	117

THE 1953 SEASON

Mickey O'Neil returned as the Generals' manager in 1953. Over the winter, he helped secure a working agreement with the Cincinnati Reds, the first and only major league affiliation the club ever had. In fact, for the first time in Kitty League history, all eight clubs had affiliations with a major league club: Union City with the Brooklyn Dodgers, Hopkinsville with the Philadelphia Athletics, Fulton with the Washington Senators, Madisonville with the Chicago White Sox, Owensboro with the New York Yankees, and Paducah with the St. Louis Cardinals. The Reds' minor league director, Bill McKechnie Jr., sent two other farm clubs, Burlington, Iowa of the Class B Three-I League and Ogden, Utah of the Class C Pioneer League, to Jackson for spring training. Ogden trained with the Generals at Municipal Park while Burlington practiced at Death Valley on Union University's campus. Burlington's manager was former Cincinnati right-hander Johnny Vander Meer, who hurled two consecutive no-hitters for the Reds in 1938. He pitched three innings of relief in an exhibition game against the Generals on April 3, allowing only one hit.

With the exception of veteran catcher Dominic Italiano and limited-service center fielder Lonnie Eastham, the Generals' roster was comprised entirely of rookies with no professional experience. When asked about his young ballclub, O'Neil remarked, "I had rather they learn it my way." The veteran manager was optimistic about his team's chances and, with the exception of needing an additional infielder, felt that it was "pretty well set and [we]expect to be in the race."

Generals Fact
In 1953, the Generals were a Class D team for the Cincinnati Reds, the only time in team history that it had a working agreement with a major league club.

Although inexperienced and at times inconsistent during the season, the pitching staff had several promising young hurlers. Three of them—Ray D'Agrosa, Howard Whitson, and Earl Gearhardt—won in double figures and completed 13 games each. The left-handed D'Agrosa led the team with 14 victories while using a blazing sidearm fastball for 158 strikeouts. Hard-throwing right-hander Howard Whitson was the workhorse of the staff, logging the most innings pitched (191) and appearances (33) with a 13-12 record and 3.72 ERA. Earl Gearhart was second on the staff in innings pitched (184) and finished at 10-13. Right-hander Carroll Drostie had the best curveball on the staff, but a lack on control led to a team-high 12 wild pitches, 94 walks, and a 9-9 record. The only Tennesseann the club, Ivan "Hambone" Mills had 129 strikeouts (second behind D'Agrosa) but the tall right-hander finished at 7-12 with a 5.69 ERA. Ritchie Roth, a 6' 7" right-hander from Pleasantville, New Jersey, showed the most potential coming out of spring training with a blazing fastball, a good curve, and great control.

SLEEVE PATCH WORN BY THE PLAYERS TO COMMEMORATE THE 50TH ANNIVERSARY OF THE KITTY LEAGUE

The 1953 Generals at the start of the season. (Left to right) Top row: Carroll Drostie, Eddie Miller, Juan Corrillo, Ivan Mills, Hiram Hopper (club owner), Roland Huss, Larry Rowley, Ray D'Agrosa, Ritchie Roth. Bottom row: Lonnie Eastham, Lloyd Burgess, John Husick, Howard Whitson, Mickey O'Neil (manager), Dominic Italiano, Joe Daidone, Dick Kolomay. Foreground: Jim Bailey (batboy).

But the 18-year-old developed bone chips in his elbow that kept him sidelined for a month and limited him to only 16 games, compiling a 3-2 mark with a 5.43 ERA.

The rookie Generals opened the season at home on May 1 against their traditional Opening Day rivals, the Union City Dodgers. Team owner Hiram Hopper tried to make Municipal Park more fan-friendly with the addition of bleachers along the left and right field lines and a new concession stand beneath the grandstand. Union City scored 10 runs in the first three innings off four Jackson hurlers, but the Generals responded with eight tallies in the next three to make it 10-8. Their offense was shut down the rest of the game by Dodgers righthander Tom Sheridan as his teammates fashioned a larger lead to win 15-8. The series moved to Union City, where left-hander Earl Gordon struck out 17 Generals en route to an 8-3 victory, and the Dodgers completed the sweep with a 10-6 win the next day.

Just six games into the season, the Generals lost their hustling center fielder, Lonnie Eastham, who fractured his shoulder while making a shoestring catch. He returned three weeks later but the injury affected his hitting and throwing arm, forcing his release in mid-June after hitting only .225 in 22 games.

Jackson fell into the league cellar after losing 11 of their first 14 games of the season. The club rebounded somewhat the rest of May, winning 10 of their last 14 to end the month in sixth place, only two games below .500 and 2½ games behind the first-place Madisonville Miners. They dropped two high-scoring contests to the Kentucky club within a week, losing

19-2 at home on May 23 and 26-3 a week later at Madisonville. The second game, the nightcap of a Memorial Day doubleheader, saw four Jackson pitchers yield 27 hits.

With the team struggling through yet another second division season, local fans had little interest in coming to the games and once again there was a mid-season financial crisis. Ticket sales were just enough to cover the players' meal allowances and travel expenses with nothing left over. The team managed to pay their salaries and other expenses from the sale of advertisements on the outfield fence and on the scorecards through the first two months of the season. When Hiram Hopper was unable to meet the July 1 payroll, the team met and discussed the situation. "We had a meeting and a couple of players didn't want to play," remembered pitcher Howard Whitson. "The farm director, Bill McKechnie, showed up and he joined our meeting. He guaranteed that the Reds would pick up our salaries and that kind of passed by and we went out and played."

Generals Fact
The Generals almost had a player strike after owner Hiram Hopper missed payroll on July 1, but the Cincinnati Reds promised them they would receive their salaries.

The first game of a June 17 doubleheader with Fulton was interrupted by league president Shelby Peace, who told the fans in attendance about the team's financial situation and encouraged better turnouts for future games to keep professional baseball in town. He estimated that it would take an average attendance of 600 per game in order for the club to break even, even though they were typically drawing less than half that number. He also announced the beginning of a ticket-selling campaign with books of 20 tickets sold for $10 each. Hopper felt that it would take 300-400 books sold to carry the team through the remainder of the season.

The Generals began the month of July in seventh place, eight games behind league-leading Madisonville and only a half-game away from falling back into the cellar. Though they lost nine of their first 15 games, two of their victories came at the wrong time for the Miners. The two teams faced one another in the July 4 doubleheader at Municipal Park. The Kentuckians had since fallen into second place behind Fulton but were only a half-game behind with the chance to reclaim the league lead and host the Kitty League All-Star Game later in the month. But the Generals' starting pitching held them to 10 hits in both contests. Right-hander Howard Whitson gave up only four hits in the first game and retired the side in all but two innings of the seven-inning contest to win 6-1. Carroll Drostie took the ball under the lights and set the Miners down in the second game, 4-3, allowing Fulton to retain first place and host the All-Star Game on July 19.

First baseman Charles "Chick" Re's two-run homer was the difference in the Generals' 6-4 victory over the Union City Dodgers on July 14, and sparked a six-game winning streak (their longest of the season) that put them in sixth place and only three games below .500. They scored 48 runs during the streak as their pitching and defense held the opposition to 21 runs. Left-hander Ray D'Agrosa's sidearm fastball baffled the Paducah Chiefs three days later as they struck out 17 times and made contact on only four hits. The 19-year-old Bronx, New York native fanned at least one batter in all but one inning's work and set down the side in the ninth to win 4-1. His teammates took advantage of four fielding miscues to score all their unearned tallies. The next day, right-hander Carroll Drostie struck out 11 and, though he showed some wildness with six walks, yielded only seven hits to beat the Chiefs 14-7.

The 1953 Generals at the end of the season. (Left to right) Top row: Earl Gearhardt, Vince Monaco, Bill Newkirk, Ray D'Agrosa, George McLeod, Ivan Mills, Jerry Elder, John Scercy. Bottom row: Ritchie Roth, Howard Whitson, Chick Re, Eddie Miller, Mickey O'Neil (manager), Gene Bennett, Carroll Drostie, Dick Wehman, Dominic Italiano. Foreground: Eric Oman (mascot), Jim Bailey (batboy).

Even though they were 12 games out of first, the Generals were only a half-game out of fourth and the first division going into a three-game series with the league-leading Fulton Lookouts at Municipal Park on July 22. The hard-hitting Kentuckians crushed their hopes by winning all three games, though two of them were by close margins. Fulton ace Bob Sherman limited Jackson to three hits in the final game to win 8-1.

During the game, Jackson shortstop Eddie Miller nailed Fulton slugger Ned Waldrop in the face while firing the ball to first as the big first baseman slid into second trying to break up a double play. "He (Miller) was getting banged around constantly on double plays. They were just hammering him," teammate Howard Whitson recalled. "Mickey kept telling him, 'Until you start throwing low and get those guys out of your way, they're going to kill you down there.'" Unfortunately for Waldrop, he was the When Miller finally heeded O'Neil's advice, the result was Waldrop being sent to the hospital with a broken jaw and Miller being out of action for a few days with an injured hand. "After that," Whitson laughed, "they started getting down and Eddie had a better life."

The Generals got even with the league leaders by taking two games from the Lookouts at Fulton's Fairfield Park July 24 and 25. Right-hander Ivan (Hambone) Mills tossed a three-hitter with eight strikeouts in the second game to win 4-2 and almost had a grand slam home run at the plate. The Loudon, Tennessee native connected for what should have been a bases loaded clout in the second inning, but in the midst of his celebratory trip around the bags, he failed to touch second base. The Fulton shortstop took notice, called for the new ball, and stepped on second for the out. Mills received a tongue-lashing from Manager O'Neil when he returned to the dugout.

Jackson broke into the first division for the first time all season after winning six of their first nine games in August to gain a fourth-place tie with the Mayfield Clothiers. But the Fulton Lookouts once again deflated the Generals' aspirations by taking the first two games of a three-game series at Municipal Park, 16-6 and 6-0, and driving them back into sixth place. But Howard Whitson tossed a three-hitter in the third game and John Scercy, the team's leading home run hitter, drove a letter-high curveball over the fence for a two-run blast to win the final game, 6-1.

The Generals traveled to Madisonville, where they took two out of three, but their pitching staff was pounded into submission with back-to-back onslaughts at Mayfield, 18-10 and 26-2, on August 15 and 16. Clothiers manager Austin Knickerbocker continued his season-long home run habit against Jackson, hitting a three-run blast in the first game and a two-run shot in the third. The Generals won their next three, all come-from-behind victories, to slip past fifth-place Hopkinsville and gain another fourth place tie with Mayfield. But the Hoppers pummeled three Jackson hurlers for 21 hits en route to a 16-4 victory in the final game to push both Jackson and Mayfield out of the first division and into fifth place.

With only a week left in the season, the battered Generals made a last-ditch effort to break into the first division and gain a playoff berth. They swept a two-game series at Fulton on August 21 and 22, then took one out of two at home against Union City. Jackson held a precarious one-run lead at Owensboro on August 25 when they loaded the bases in the seventh inning with no outs. Mid-season addition Jerry Elder hit a ground ball to the Oilers' shortstop, who quickly fired home with enough time to tag Gene Bennett coming to the plate. But Bennett was able to knock the ball out of the catcher's glove and score and as the Owensboro backstop scrambled for the ball, Dick Wehman scored right behind him to give the Generals a more comfortable 7-4 lead. Lefty Ray D'Agrosa starred both on the mound and at the plate, holding the Oilers to six hits on nine strikeouts, fanning the side in the ninth for the win and hitting a two-run homer in the second inning. The victory elevated the Generals into fourth place, though only a single percentage point ahead of Mayfield with two games left in the season.

Hopkinsville did their part to help Jackson's cause the next day, beating Mayfield 12-6, but Owensboro ace John Pfautz handcuffed the Generals, allowing only five hits while his teammates ran roughshod over four Generals' hurlers for a 7-1 victory. The loss dropped Jackson into fifth, though still only a half game away from a possible playoff spot going into the final game of the season. But to ensure a

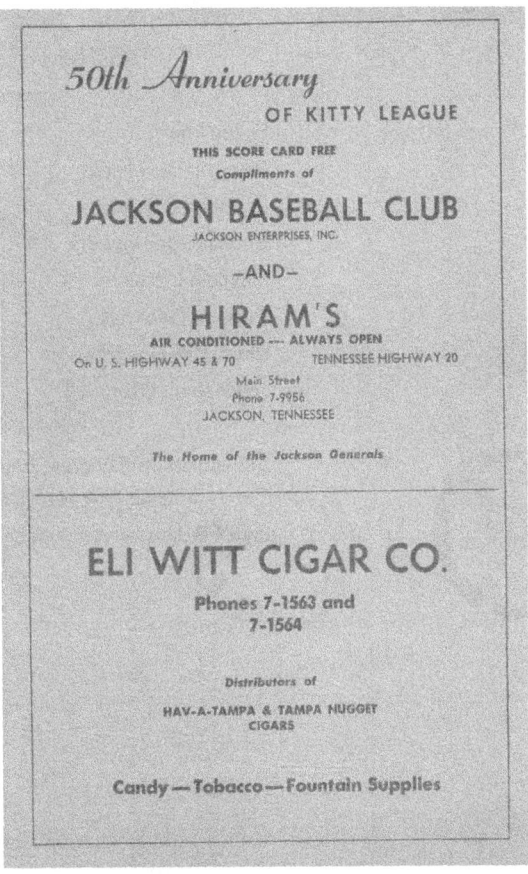

1953 GENERALS SCORECARD COVER

fourth-place finish, both Hopkinsville and Mayfield had to lose their final games.

Some 700 Jackson fans came to Municipal Park to see the season finale against the third place Paducah Chiefs, who were already assured of a playoff berth. The Kentuckians scored four runs in the second and third innings off Howard Whitson, but the 18-year-old right-hander shut them down the next three before giving way to reliever Ray D'Agrosa, who did the same the remainder of the game. But Paducah right-hander Chris Speas had an equally effective performance, yielding only one run in the second without the threat of an uprising until the bottom of the ninth. The Generals managed to get two hits and a walk to load the bases for their leading hitter, outfielder Gene Bennett. With two outs and the team's playoff hopes on the line, he ended the season with a fly ball to left and the Generals suffered a 4-1 defeat. Afterward the fans in attendance collected $100 for the players in appreciation for their efforts during the season and gave manager Mickey O'Neil a rousing ovation.

The team finished in sixth place with a record of 58-62, 12 games behind the Fulton Lookouts, who won their third consecutive Kitty League pennant. League sportswriters and broadcasters rewarded the efforts of Mickey O'Neil, who led a rookie squad to a near first-division finish, by naming him Manager of the Year, edging out Madisonville skipper Everett Robinson by one vote.

1953 Kitty League Standings

Fulton Lookouts	70	50	.583	—
Madisonville Miners	67	53	.558	3
Paducah Chiefs	67	53	.558	3
Hopkinsville Hoppers	59	60	.496	10.5
Mayfield Clothiers	58	61	.487	11.5
Jackson Generals	58	62	.483	12
Union City Dodgers	51	69	.425	19
Owensboro Oilers	49	71	.408	21

Shaughnessy playoffs—Fulton beat Hopkinsville 3 games to 1 and Paducah beat Madisonville two games to none.

Finals—Paducah defeated Fulton 3 games to none

1954

Finish	Record	Pct.	GB
Eighth*	(1-41)	.024	—

* Jackson franchise returned to the Kitty League with a 1-26 record on June 1. League adopted a split-season schedule and the remainder of Jackson's games were forfeited to their scheduled opponents.

Manager	Record	Pct.
Lou Lukasiuk (Lucas)	(1-26)	.037

Attendance	Lg Rank
3,700	Ninth

Starting Lineup

C	Stewart Riles	.340 BA
1B	William (Bill) Hughes	.291 BA
2B	Daniel (Danny) Meyers	.359 BA
3B	Vance Byrd	.286 BA
SS	Lou Lukasiuk (Lucas)	.405 BA
LF	Mike Luciano	.286 BA
CF	Mike Milinazzo	.271 BA
RF	Harry Arterburn	.262 BA

Pitching Staff

RH	Richard Hardish	(1-4)
LH	Charles Dillion	(0-4)
RH	John Strunk	(0-4)
LH	James (Jim) Kluck	(0-6)

Top 10 Batters and Top 5 Pitchers

Batter	BA	G	AB	R	H	2B	3B	HR	RBI	SB
Lou Lucas	.405	15	42	5	17	3	1	0	9	1
Danny Meyers*	.326	89	359	68	117	13	2	1	23	8
Stewart Riles**	.298	28	84	19	25	2	4	0	17	2
Bill Hughes#	.288	83	274	50	79	15	5	3	51	5
Vance Byrd	.286	23	84	12	24	3	1	0	11	1
Michael Luciano	.286	15	56	14	16	3	0	1	11	1
Mike Milinazzo	.271	25	85	16	23	4	0	1	9	0
Harry Arterburn	.262	26	107	11	28	7	2	1	13	0
Joe Jones	.189	10	37	3	7	0	0	0	4	1
Charles Perkins	.182	13	44	6	8	1	0	0	6	0

Pitcher	ERA	G	IP	W	L	CG	ER	Sh	BB	SO
Richard Hardish	7.26	9	37.2	1	4	1	—	0	21	17
Jim Kluck##	9.62	12	58	0	6	1	—	0	18	20
Charles Dillon	12.93	5	18.1	0	4	0	—	0	13	6
Vance Byrd	13.03	5	15.2	0	1	0	—	0	12	20
John Strunk	14.61	6	27.1	0	4	0	—	0	25	10

* Played 63 games with Fulton Lookouts ** Played 3 games with Hopkinsville and 6 with Fulton
\# Also with the Hopkinsville Hoppers \#\# Also pitched with Central City Reds

During the last game of the 1953 season, team owner Hiram Hopper announced to the hometown crowd that he could no longer continue to operate the Generals, but hoped to sell the club to another local individual or group that would keep it in Jackson. Efforts were made during the off-season to take the struggling Kitty League franchise off his hands, with local contractor and realtor Ira Johnson leading the effort. It was hoped that the team could be operated as a non-profit civic venture like other Kitty League cities, but more discussion than action took place and nothing materialized. "We in Jackson should be utterly ashamed of ourselves," Congressman Tom Murray said, "if we allow organized baseball to leave the city." A committee consisting of Johnson, Murray, Marlin Allen, Dr. Henry Herron, Steve Stein, Commissioner Chester Parham, Kathleen Allen, John Knight, Edd Topp, and *Jackson Sun* sports editor John D. Graham was created to find a way to fund the purchase. Nothing came of the effort to meet Hopper's $7,800 asking price and Clarksville and Dyersburg's interest waned in the winter months.

Despite saying that he would not operate the Generals in 1954, Hopper rescinded and tried one last time to continue professional baseball in Jackson. He hired Peter R. Mucci, former general manager of the Jamestown, New York club of the Class D PONY League, as the Generals' business manager. Mucci, with the assistance of members of the Junior Chamber of Commerce, initiated a preseason ticket drive from Hiram's Restaurant in mid April to sell 20-game books for the discounted price of $10 each, with anyone buying two getting the third for free. The team also offered free admission to children under 12 who were accompanied by an adult.

The 1954 Generals lost their first 26 games of the season and came within a game of tying the Kitty League record for consecutive losses. Their pursuit of the record brought national media attention to the Generals, but it also helped bring about the end of professional baseball in Jackson.

The team was on shaky financial ground after two disappointing seasons both in the win-loss column and at the gate. When Hiram Hopper bought the Generals in 1952, he optimistically felt he could make the team a financial success within two years. But two second division finishes and a continually declining attendance cost him $6,500 after purchasing the club for $10,000. Still he decided to give it one more try in 1954, hoping to collect $20,000 from the sale of 1,000 advance season ticket books and give the club a preseason financial boost. Despite the efforts of supporters such as E.L. Womack, an enthusiastic fan who alone sold $400 worth of books, only 50 books at less than $1,000 were purchased.

Generals Fact

The Generals lost their first 26 games of the 1954 season. At the time, it was believed they broke the Kitty League record of 25 set by the 1922 Paducah Indians. Research shows Paducah actually lost 27 straight games.

The Generals found no solace in the weather as rain and unseasonably cold temperatures hampered their spring training workouts at Municipal Park. Although the other Kitty League clubs experienced the same difficulties, their players had the opportunity to practice under the warm Florida sun for several weeks at the major league camps.

New manager Lou Lucas, a former St. Louis Cardinals farmhand, utilized what little time he had before Opening Day. He wanted "a hustling, running club" and set up a sliding pit at Municipal Park to instruct his young players on base running fundamentals. For the second consecutive season, the roster consisted of rookies and a few limited service players with at least 90 days in professional ball. The Superior (Wisconsin) Blues of the Class C Northern League, who held their workouts at Municipal Park several weeks before the Generals reported, left four unsigned players to try out for Jackson. Two of them, second baseman Dan Meyers and shortstop Mike Milinazzo, made the team.

What Lucas could surmise in the abbreviated spring workouts was his club's lack of quality pitching and offense. Because the Generals had lost their working agreement with the Cincinnati Reds over the winter, the club could no longer rely on players sent in from a major league farm system and were forced to resume their independent status, finding players where they could.

Lucas began the season with veteran Bill Hughes at first base; 20-year-old Dan Meyers at second; Frank Martinez, a Detroit Tigers prospect, at third; Mike Milinazzo at short; Jeff Hopper in left field; rifle-armed Harry Arterburn in center; John Zawacki in right; and Tom Giordano catching. The pitching staff included Richard Hardish, veteran Jim Kluck (who was returning from two years' service in the Korean War), Charles Dillon, Ed Pratt, Stan Kovaleski, Bob Huff, Sonny Wilson, and Thomas Lee Mills. Lucas played part-time at shortstop and as a relief pitcher.

The season had a foretelling beginning on May 4 as the Union City Dodgers dominated the Generals 20-0 behind the pitching of Jim Majors. The left-hander allowed only two hits, a double by Frank Martinez and a single by Danny Meyers, and struck out 16 batters. Nineteen-year-old Richard Hardish started for Jackson but never made it out of the first inning; two walks, a hit, and two errors that scored four runs prematurely ended his professional debut. Three relievers followed, but made matters worse by giving up 13 more hits and 16 more runs. Right-hander Jim Kluck, who took over for Hardish, allowed 12 runs and 10 hits by himself in six-and-one-third innings of work.

The team returned to Municipal Park the next evening for their home opener, where the Greyhound hitters took up where they left off. They pounded 19 hits off three Jackson hurlers, whose generosity included 15 free passes to first base. The Generals' defense fared no better, committing 10 costly errors to contribute to their 24-1 defeat. Jackson was baffled by another Union City pitcher, Tom Sheridan, whose sidearm delivery yielded only two hits. The Generals' only run came on a fielder's choice.

Generals Fact
The Generals started their streak with losses in their first two games of the season to the Union City Dodgers, 20-0 and 24-1, on May 4 and 5, 1954.

After the game, Lucas released pitchers Bob Huff and Stan Kovaleski, catcher John Zawacki, and outfielders Chuck McMillan and Bill Simmons. During the next few weeks, roster changes were made almost daily as he searched for a winning combination. Among those acquired during the process were right-handers James Carswell and Robert Morehouse, pitcher-shortstop Vance Byrd, and catchers Stewart Riles and Charles Perkins. But the horrible pitching, fielding miscues, and poor hitting continued and the team continued to lose.

The Generals never enjoyed a lead until May 12, when they surprised themselves by edging ahead of the Owensboro Oilers, 2-0, in the first five innings. But the Kentuckians scored a run in the third and three in the sixth to take a 4-2 lead, then added four more to send Jackson to its ninth consecutive loss, 8-2.

Two days later Jackson pushed ahead 5-0 in the first game of a doubleheader with the Oilers. Starting pitcher Jack Strunk's double and center fielder Mike Milinazzo's two-run homer brought four runs across in the second inning. Another was added in the fourth on shortstop Vance Byrd's single. But the lead crumbled on a bases loaded triple by Owensboro in the sixth and four runs in the last two innings that gave them an 8-5 win. The Oilers took an 11-2 lead in the second game, then purposely made outs with their hitters at the plate to squeeze in five innings of play before the Sunday curfew ended the contest. One of Owensboro's prospects was shortstop Tony Kubek, who went on to play with the New York Yankees and later became a broadcaster. The young Kubek, in his first season of professional ball in 1954, played three games at Jackson's Municipal Park and hit two triples in two games.

On May 13, the Jackson *Sun* reported that the Generals had signed a working agreement with the Chicago Cubs. The Cubs would supply them with players from their organization and had supposedly sent two scouts to evaluate the team. But the announcement made by Generals business manager Pete Mucci was premature; the Cubs had only expressed an interest in sending the team a few surplus players. It was rumored that the deal fell through due to the Cincinnati Reds' bad report to Chicago on their dealings with Hiram Hopper the year before.

The Generals' bats came alive on May 19 as they touched the Fulton Lookouts for 15 hits. They collected at least 10 hits in their next eight games, but poor pitching and costly errors jinxed their chances to end the dreadful losing streak.

The team tied what was believed to be the modern consecutive loss record of 18 games set by the 1937 Paducah Indians without ever taking the field. They left Jackson at one o'clock in the morning for Madisonville, Kentucky on May 22, where a three-game series against the Miners was scheduled. Three hours later, the radiator broke down. Lucas telephoned Jackson for a second bus, but was told to have theirs fixed. Repairs did not begin until noon and were not finished until late in the afternoon. At 7:55 that evening, Lucas called the Madisonville officials from Hopkinsville, just thirty-five miles away, hoping that the game could be postponed. League president Shelby Peace instead delayed its start until 9:15. Twenty minutes later, the team resumed their journey; thirty minutes later, the headlights went out. The bus cautiously made it to the next town, Crofton, where Lucas telephoned Madisonville again, asking for more reliable transportation. Instead the umpires declared the game forfeited to the Miners, 9-0. At 1:30 in the morning, some twenty hours and 160 miles after their journey began, a truck picked up the exhausted Generals and took them the rest of the way.

Jackson *Sun* sports editor John D. Graham tried to put a positive spin on the futile Generals' season. "Lucas is making the best of what he has and is correct in stating that he has a hustling ball club," he wrote on May 16. "Even in defeat, Jackson has never stopped hustling. This is more than we can say of some winning ball clubs that we have seen."

Generals Fact
A broken radiator and headlight failure on the team bus led to a forfeit by the Generals and their 18th consecutive loss on May 22, 1954.

A typical night game at Municipal Park in 1954. Notice the sparse fans in the grandstand.

As the Generals drew closer to the supposed all-time Kitty League record for consecutive losses (which the press erroneously reported as being 25 games set by Paducah in 1922), they drew the attention of sports media outside Jackson. Feature stories about the team were published in the *Nashville Banner* and in *The Sporting News*. The *St. Louis Post-Dispatch* carried two full pages of photos, using the club to depict the struggles of lower minor league baseball. "The publicity may not have been of the most enjoyable variety," Graham noted, "but at least the rest of the baseball public knows that Jackson had a team."

In the final days of May there were hints that the Generals might not survive the month, much less the rest of the season. Attendance at Municipal Park was even more scarce than usual, which meant that Hiram Hopper had very little money to improve the team or keep it afloat. Their comical trip to Madisonville might never have taken place had Hopper not been persuaded to keep the team going, at least until Memorial Day, which traditionally was a high-attendance doubleheader. When the Generals ventured out of town for a three-game series at Fulton, the Lookouts management agreed to pay their travel and lodging expenses, normally the responsibility of the visiting club. With another road series scheduled at Mayfield, Kentucky beginning on June 1, it seemed certain that the Generals would not last much longer.

Jackson hosted Madisonville in the Memorial Day doubleheader on May 31. They went into the series supposedly tied for the record, having lost their twenty-fifth game at Fulton, 10-9. Right-hander Jim Kluck took the mound in the first game and held the Miners scoreless through the first three innings. His teammates scored a run in the second to take an early lead, but Kluck weakened in the fourth and allowed six hits (including two home runs) that made it 6-1. Relievers James Carswell and Gerald McGhay held Madisonville scoreless until the ninth, but Jackson's hitters could manage only three more runs off three Miner hurlers and lost 7-5.

(At the time, the players and the sports media believed the Generals had broken the Kitty League record for consecutive losses, thought to be 25 games set by the Paducah Indians in 1922. Research of the daily box scores that season has revealed this was not the case. Paducah instead lost 27 consecutive games from August 7 to September 2, 1922, and finished the second-half of that season with a record of 8-50.)

In the second game of the Memorial Day doubleheader, Jackson's pitching and hitting came together effectively for the first time all season. Right-hander Richard Hardish held the Miners to four hits in eight innings' work and the Generals' offense dominated Madisonville's pitchers. Consecutive doubles by Vance Byrd, Mike Milinazzo, and Harry Arterburn scored three runs in the third and after six more innings, the Generals were leading 10-0. Hardish was generous in the ninth, giving up three singles that brought two runs in, but amazingly, Jackson held on to the lead and, after 26 consecutive defeats, tasted victory for the first time all season, 10-2.

But there was little time for celebration and no chance to capitalize on their newfound success. The next morning, June 1, Hopper announced that he was returning the franchise to the Kitty League. "I cannot continue putting good money with bad money," he rationalized. Lucas wanted to play one last game at Municipal Park, with the gate receipts given to the players. But Madisonville manager Bob Latshaw refused to play unless two banks of lights were replaced, which the Jackson owner could not afford to do. The league assumed the contracts of 10 Jackson players and released the rest. The Generals' remaining 15 games of the first-half were forfeited and they officially finished with a 1-41 record and a .024 winning percentage.

Kitty League president Shelby Peace and league officials hurried to find a city that would take the abandoned team, but found no takers. The Chicago Cubs reportedly agreed to sign a working agreement with the new owner as further incentive for accepting the club and the league voted to create a split-season schedule to give it a fresh start. The franchise was offered to Dyersburg, Paris, and Clarksville, Tennessee and Bowling Green and Henderson, Kentucky, but each declined. It appeared that Milan, Tennessee might accept it, but opted not to at the last minute. Peace even considered making the Generals exclusively a "road" team, playing all of their games without a home field.

Eventually the team was accepted by Central City, Kentucky and renamed the Reds. But new surroundings and a new name failed to bring success to the plagued franchise. The Reds finished the second-half with a 12-44 record and Central City did not host another team the next season. The Kitty League itself folded for the fifth and final time in 1955.

1954 Kitty League Standings

First Half (May 4-July 4)

Team	W	L	Pct.	GB
Union City Dodgers	47	17	.712	—
Mayfield Clothiers	37	22	.627	5
Fulton Lookouts	35	24	.593	7
Hopkinsville Hoppers	31	29	.593	11.5
Owensboro Oilers	29	28	.509	12
Madisonville Miners	26	32	.448	15.5
Paducah Chiefs	24	32	.429	16.5
Jackson Generals*	1	41	.024	x

Second Half (July 5-August 30)

Team	W	L	Pct.	GB
Madisonville Miners	35	20	.636	—
Owensboro Oilers	36	21	.632	—
Union City Dodgers	34	23	.596	2
Fulton Lookouts	34	23	.596	2
Hopkinsville Hoppers	27	30	.474	9
Mayfield Clothiers	27	30	.474	9
Paducah Chiefs	21	35	.375	14.5
Central City Reds**	12	44	.214	23.5

* Team owner Hiram Hopper returned the franchise to the Kitty League with a 1-26 record on June 1. The league adopted a split-season format and the remainder of Jackson's games were forfeited to their scheduled opponents.

** Jackson franchise transferred to Central City, Kentucky for the second-half. (The team was not affiliated with the Cincinnati Reds.)

Split-season playoff—Union City defeated Madisonville 4 games to two.

Baseball is Back

The 1950s was a difficult decade for minor league baseball marked by declining attendance, as Americans enjoyed the modern conveniences of indoor air conditioning and watched major league games on television or listened to them on the radio. More people owned automobiles and often drove 260 miles to watch the St. Louis Cardinals rather than pay a 65-cent general admission ticket to see the Generals at home. A writer for the *St. Louis Post-Dispatch* observed one spring evening in 1954 when the local drive-in theatre was packed and several hundred spectators watched the Little League games, while only 53 fans showed up for a Generals game. The paid attendance could not even take care of the electric bill.

Municipal Park was a makeshift ballpark located at the West Tennessee State Fairgrounds, which was inaccessible for many fans because city buses and taxis did not run that far from downtown. It was also a bad place to watch a game. "Even on a reasonable warm night, all that Forked Deer [River] moisture would settle in down there and you would have to wear jackets in the summer," former sportswriter John D. Graham recalled. "It wasn't like going out in shirt sleeves to a ballgame." As a result, the outfield would be covered in a blanket of fog. The grandstand was not configured for baseball and made it hard for fans on each end to watch. In addition to the mosquitoes, they also had to endure the smell of burning garbage from the city dump beyond the right field fence.

Almost from the start, the Generals in the 1950s suffered from low attendance. The local Baseball Association would threaten each season to return the franchise to the Kitty League, but each time crowds increased just enough to satisfy the owners and encourage them to put more funds into the club. When the Association finally reached its financial limit in 1952, local businessman Hiram Hopper saved the team from leaving town and hoped local community leaders and fans would support the team and keep professional baseball in Jackson. Fans who grew up cheering for the winning Generals teams of the 1940s attributed the lack of fan interest to the lack of competitive teams in the Fifties. "In Jackson, you've got to have a winner to draw," one fan said. "You have to win practically every game. I've noticed that in other [local] sports."

The final event that sealed the Generals' fate was the construction of a new ballpark at Death Valley (located at the end of College Street) for the city's Babe Ruth League teams. A widespread community effort backed the project, with the Junior Chamber of Commerce acquiring the funds and local contractors donating their services for its construction. With all the enthusiasm for the Babe Ruth League teams, there was none left for the struggling Generals. Their 26-game losing streak simply hastened the inevitable in 1954. Four years earlier, *Jackson Sun* sportswriter Jimmy Hamlin wrote prophetically that "if and when professional baseball departs from Jackson, she'll be gone a long time."

Pursuit of a Team

INDEED IT WAS a long time—45 years—before Jackson hosted another team. Over the next three decades, minor league baseball struggled with much the same problems that Generals owner Hiram Hopper faced. With escalating major-league player salaries, high ticket and concession prices, and the ever-present threat of labor strife in the 1980s, fans rekindled their love for the game through the minor leagues. Families could attend a minor-league game for significantly less money and enjoy seats much closer to the field than they could afford at a major-league ballpark. Teams marketed themselves aggressively and created fun and unusual promotions to draw fans. By 1990, there were 200 minor-league teams across the country where only 130 had existed 17 years earlier.

That year, Jackson Mayor Charles Farmer led the city's effort to bring baseball back. In early September, Mike Nicklous, principal owner of the Memphis Chicks, offered to relocate his Double-A Southern League franchise to Jackson. The Parks and Recreation Department proposed building a new ballpark at the West Tennessee State Fairgrounds (former home of the Generals) as part of the city's renovation project there. Nicklous, however, preferred a site alongside Interstate 40 near Christmasville Road. In anticipation of the move, the City Council unanimously approved a joint venture with Madison County to build a 7,500-seat ballpark for $3.5 million.

It was Nicklous' intention to relocate the Chicks to Jackson is he gained approval to move another team he owned, the Edmondton Trappers of the Triple-A Pacific Coast League, to Memphis and switch it to another Triple-A league, the American Association. This would give him the unique opportunity to own two minor-league teams just 80 miles apart. But the other Triple-A owners unanimously voted down his proposal and the deal with Jackson collapsed. A year later, he approached potential local investors about purchasing a majority interest in the Chicks, but nothing came of it.

Generals Fact
After the demise of the Generals in 1954, it took 45 years for pro baseball to return to Jackson.

In June 1992, Jackson was one of 13 cities vying for a Double-A expanison team when the Florida Marlins and the Colorado Rockies were added to the major leagues. A month later, Southern League president Jimmy Bragan, impressed with the city's determination to get a team, offered Jackson the first opportunity to purchase the Charlotte Knights after that city received a Triple-A franchise. But there was a catch: Local investors had to provide a letter of credit for $3.8 million in 10 days or the offer would be withdrawn.

While preparations were made to quickly break ground on the proposed ballpark site, Mayor Farmer and leading investor Chuck Clark hurriedly tried to put together an ownership group and secure the needed funds before the July 24 deadline. But lacking a single significant backer and no interest outside Madison County in the effort, the mayor grudgingly admitted defeat one day before the deadline. Jackson's inability to gather together a solid ownership group also hurt its chances at one of the expansion clubs. "Unless we identify the heavy hitter in the future," Farmer said, "it's a waste of time to pursue it."

The City of Jackson renewed its pursuit of a team in the spring of 1996 with two more expansion franchises available at the end of the year. Chuck Clark agreed to invest $6 million into the club and serve as principal owner if 3,600 season-tickets were sold. Despite falling short of the mark, the city optimistically filed its application for one of the expansion teams alsongs with a $15,000 non-refundable fee on August 1. Their hopes sank when Clark dropped out, leaving them without an owner as they prepared to make their presentation to the expansion committee later in the month. Although Mayor Farmer initially chose not to do so, Southern League president Arnie Fielkow (a member of the committee) encouraged him to ask for an extension and make the city's presentation in October, allowing time to find another prospective owner.

Meanwhile, 80 miles away, David Hersh, president and general manager of the Memphis Chicks, struggled to gain support from Memphis and Shelby County officials for the construction of a new ballpark. Despite being in the largest market in the Southern League, the team suffered declining attendance in 33-year-old Tim McCarver Stadium, a facility that no longer met the standards of minor league baseball.

In early September 1996, Hersh met with Mayor Farmer about the possibility of relocating the Chicks to Jackson. Lawyers on both sides spent two weeks working out an agreement, which was approved by the Jackson City Council on September 24 by a 6-2 vote (with one absent). Hersh proclaimed to the Memphis media, "We're going to Jackson because Jackson is action. Memphis is discussion. Memphis is words. All we've heard is words."

But obstacles arose from Memphis and the Southern League. Memphis businessman Dean Jernigan tried unsuccessfully to purchase the Chicks and keep them in the city, then shifted his focus on securing a Triple-A expansion team. With Southern League approval of the move set in mid January 1997, league president Arnie Fielkow stipulated that the Chicks had to pay a $1.1 million "relocation" fee as compensation for the league losing its best market. The matter eventually resolved itself when Memphis was awarded an expansion franchise on January 14—which became the Memphis Redbirds—and Hersh and Jernigan each agreed to pay half of the "relocation" fee.

THE DIAMOND JAXX

PREPARATIONS WERE MADE quickly for the construction of Jackson's new ballpark off Interstate 40 southeast of Exit 85. In February 1997, the city signed a contract with Heery International, a design-build construction management company that specialized in sports facilities. It agreed to build a 6,000-seat ballpark for $8 million and have it ready for Opening Day on April 16, 1998.

The *Jackson Sun* sponsored a "Name the Team" contest with four season tickets for five years offered for the winning entry. Over 1,500 suggestions were narrowed down to three choices: the Diamond Jacks, Mad Jacks, and Boom (reflecting the city's economic upswing). A telephone poll of newspaper readers decided upon the name Diamond Jacks suggested by Jackson resident Jane Des Ormeaux. After a logo was created, the name officially became the West Tenn Diamond Jaxx.

In October, the Diamond Jaxx became the Double-A affiliate for the Chicago Cubs with Dave Trembley as the team's first manager. (He later became manager of the Baltimore Orioles from 2007 to 2010.) The Proctor and Gamble Company, the largest industry in Madison County, acquired the naming rights for the new ballpark, which became Pringles Park.

From 1998 to 2010, the Diamond Jaxx had a 920-889 record with four division titles, six playoff appearances, and the Southern League championship in 2000. As an affiliate of the Cubs and Seattle Mariners, 47 of their players became major-leaguers, including Kyle Farnsworth, Corey Patterson, Carlos Zambrano, Jose Molina, Mark Prior, Carlos Marmol, and Casey McGehee. Several major-leaguers on medical rehabilitation assignments also made appearances on the Diamond Jaxx's roster, the most notable being Sammy Sosa of the Cubs in 2004.

THE GENERALS RETURN

WITH A NEW ownership group in place in 2010, it was decided that a name change might reinvigorate the team among the fan base. After 13 seasons as the Diamond Jaxx, a blast from Jackson's past was announced at Pringles Park on September 6, 2010, when the new team uniforms and logo for the Jackson Generals were unveiled. From the mound, 93-year-old Jane Des Ormeaux, originator of the Diamond Jaxx name, threw the last ceremonial pitch of the Jaxx era and local business owner and former Generals pitcher Walt Mestan—wearing a replica jersey and cap from his 1950 team—threw the first pitch of the brand-new Generals era.

The 2011 Generals were affiliated with the Seattle Mariners organization. Their manager was Jim Pankovits, whose father Vince Pankovits had been player-manager of the Generals in 1952. (Jim had also managed the Jackson Generals team in Mississippi in 1998 and 1999.) The team had an impressive first-half, finishing in second place in the North Division with a record of 38-32, five games behind the Tennessee Smokies.

Pringles Park hosted the Southern League All-Star Game on June 21 and the Generals fielded seven of their own All-Stars on the North Division squad: pitchers Andrew Carraway, Jarrett Grube, Kenn Kasparek, Bobby LaFromboise, and Erasmo Ramirez, outfielder Jake Shaffer, and infielder Kyle Seager. Carraway earned the win in the North Division's 6-3 victory.

The Generals had a tougher time in the second-half of the season, highlighted by a five-game losing streak June 26-30 and a seven-game skid August 15-21. They finished in fourth place with a 30-40 record, 12-½ games behind the division champion Chattanooga Lookouts.

VINNIE CATRICALA

ANDREW CARRAWAY

There were, however, many individual achievements for the Generals. Third baseman Vinnie Catricala was named the Mariners' Minor League Player of the Year, batting .347 with 29 doubles, 11 home runs, 45 RBIs, and a .632 slugging percentage in 62 games with Jackson. Left-hander James Paxton (3-0, 1.85 ERA, 51 strikeouts in seven games) was named the league's Pitcher of the Week the first week of August and was selected to the World team in the All-Star Futures Game. Another Pitcher of the Week winner, lefty James Gillheeney (1-3, 5.49 ERA in seven games), pitched seven no-hit innings against the Suns at Jacksonville, Florida on September 3. Right-hander Andrew Carraway (9-5, 3.66 ERA, 106 strikeouts in 28 games) led the team in victories, strikeouts, and innings pitched.

GENERALS REUNION

BEFORE THE GENERALS name returned in 2011, a group of former Generals players returned to Jackson for a reunion in September 1999. Nine players and a batboy from the 1950 and 1953 teams gathered at Pringles Park to renew old friendships and share memories of seasons spent playing ball in the Kitty League.

Most had not been back to Jackson since that time and were surprised by how much the city had grown. They remembered living downtown at a boarding house run by Mrs. George Meeks or at the YMCA building on Cumberland and Lafayette Streets. "I just remember

THE 1999 GENERALS PLAYER REUNION. LEFT TO RIGHT: MIKE CONOVAN, JOHN SCERCY, CLYDE BARGER, DOMINIC ITALIANO, CARROLL DROSTIE, CHICK RE, EARL GEARHARDT, WALT MESTAN, EMIL KIRIK.

how the people of Jackson were so generous and nice," recalled former third baseman Emil Kirik. "It made a lasting impression."

Although there were players from different teams at the reunion, they all shared the common bonds of their fraternity: stories, stories, and more stories! It was a treat to listen to the all. Former pitcher Walt Mestan remembered how he convinced manager Gabby Stewart to leave him in a game against the Fulton Railroaders. He wanted to face just one more batter, he pleaded, and Stewart relented. He knew after a 3-1 count against their best hitter, Ned Waldrop, that his time was up. So he picked up the rosin bag and threw it for his last pitch. Before the umpire could raise his voice to eject him from the game, Mestan was walking to the dugout with a smile on his face.

Before going to the ballpark that evening, the players swapped stories and autographed baseballs among themselves and family members in a conference room at the Garden Plaza Hotel. Mestan rolled a ball across the table to former teammate and fellow pitcher Mike Conovan for him to sign. "That was about the same speed as your fastball," Conovan quipped. "Conovan, you couldn't break a window pane 10 feet away with your pitch," Mestan jokingly responded.

For the author, it was an opportunity to meet players he had only read about in old newspaper box scores and game accounts. This event inspired him to organize two larger reunions in Paducah, Kentucky in 2003 and Memphis in 2005 for players on other Kitty League teams. It was important for him to honor the playing careers of all these gentlemen and the joy they brought to fans in Jackson and West Tennessee from 1935 to 1954.

Former 1953 Generals (left to right): Top row: John Searcy, Earl Gearhardt, Carroll Drostie. Middle row: Dominic Italiano, Chick Re. Bottom: Jim Bailey (batboy)

Generals by the Numbers

ALL-TIME BATTING LEADERS 1935-1954

Games

1	Dick Jones	348
2	Lee Valadez	332
3	Dominic Italiano	303
4	Herbert (Dutch) Welch	299
5	Melvin (Mel) Merkel	295
6	Ernest (Ernie) Ankrom	269
7	Lou Perryman	254
8	Jesse Webb	249
9	C.C. (Cy) Miller Jr.	239
10	Grover Resigner	224

Hits

1	Dick Jones	437
2	Herbert (Dutch) Welch	338
3	Melvin (Mel) Merkel	334
4	Lee Valadez	313
5	Al Cuozzo, C.C. Miller Jr.	290
6	Ernest Ankrom	284
7	Lee Valadez	282
8	Bearl Brooks, Lou Perryman, Glen (Gabby) Stewart	258
9	Dominic Italiano	236
10	Maurice Partain	228

At-Bats

1	Dick Jones	1,414
2	Lee Valadez	1,193
3	Herbert (Dutch) Welch	1,180
4	Melvin (Mel) Merkel	1,076
5	Bearl Brooks	1,016
6	Ernest (Ernie) Ankrom	1,001
7	Louis (Lou) Perryman	960
8	Dominic Italiano	949
9	C.C. (Cy) Miller Jr.	945
10	Grover Resigner	828

Doubles

1	Herbert (Dutch) Welch	81
2	Ernest Ankrom, Dick Jones	73
3	Glen (Gabby) Stewart	71
4	Melvin (Mel) Merkel	66
5	Al Cuozzo	59
6	Lou Perryman	51
7	Dominic Italiano	49
8	Grover Resigner	46
9	Harold (Hal) Seawright	39
10	Maurice Partain	37

Runs

1	Dick Jones	251
2	Lee Valadez	233
3	Melvin (Mel) Merkel	214
4	Dominic Italiano	206
5	Herbert (Dutch) Welch	195
6	Bearl Brooks	194
7	Maurice Partain	192
8	Russell Newell	177
9	Ernest (Ernie) Ankrom	171
10	C.C. Miller Jr.	169

Triples

1	Herbert (Dutch) Welch	25
2	Al Cuozzo	20
3	Melvin (Mel) Merkel	18
4	James (Bull) Liddell	16
5	Vincent (Moon) Mullen	15
6	Lee Valadez	12
7	Ernest Ankrom, Bearl Brooks, Russell Newell, Lou Perryman	11
8	Carl Sikes, Glen Stewart	10
9	Joe Polcha	8
10	Grover Resigner	6

Home Runs

1	Melvin (Mel) Merkel	48
2	Newt (Gashouse) Parker	43
3	Al Cuozzo	34
4	Joe Polcha	27
5	Ernest (Ernie) Ankrom,	
	Harold (Hal) Seawright	25
6	Dominic Italiano, Vincent Mullen	15
7	John Scercy	14
8	Andy Scarbola	12
9	Ralph L. White	11
10	William (Buster) Morgan	9?

Strikeouts

1	Ernest (Ernie) Ankrom	166
2	Melvin (Mel) Merkel	160
3	Newt (Gashouse) Parker	142
4	Richard (Dick) Jones	126
5	Lee Valadez	125
6	Dominic Italiano	114
7	Joe Polcha	99
8	John Scercy	97
9	Vincent (Moon) Mullen	95
10	Al Cuozzo	90

Runs Batted In

1	Melvin (Mel) Merkel	198
2	Ernest Ankrom	184
3	Glen (Gabby) Stewart	178
4	Dominic Italiano	174
5	Al Cuozzo	170
6	Herbert (Dutch) Welch	161
7	Harold (Hal) Seawright	160
8	Richard (Dick) Jones	150
9	Vincent (Moon) Mullen	149
10	Newt (Gashouse) Parker	146

Stolen Bases

1	Maurice Partain	118
2	Richard (Dick) Jones	116
3	Bearl Brooks	74
4	Lee Valadez	57
5	Herbert (Dutch) Welch	42
6	C.C. (Cy) Miller Jr.	41
7	Russell Newell	38
8	Carl Sikes	37
9	Dominic Italiano, Melvin Merkel,	
	Joe Polcha	36
10	Ernest Ankrom	33

Walks

1	Dominic Italiano	252
2	Lee Valadez	227
3	Vincent (Moon) Mullen	172
4	Melvin (Mel) Merkel	162
5	Richard (Dick) Jones	159
6	Glen (Gabby) Stewart	155
7	Melvin (Mel) Merkel	133
8	Bearl Brooks	131
9	Maurice Partain	100
10	Clyde Barger	99

Batting Average (minimum 790 at-bats)

1	Herbert (Dutch) Welch	.329
2	Al Cuozzo	.326
3	Melvin (Mel) Merkel	.310
4	Richard (Dick) Jones	.309
5	C.C. (Cy) Miller Jr.	.307
6	Maurice Partain	.288
7	Ernest Ankrom	.284
8	Grover Resinger	.283
9	Louis (Lou) Perryman	.269
10	Lee Valadez	.262

All-Time Pitching Leaders 1935-1954

Wins

1	Jesse Webb	125
2	Carl Gaiser	46
3	Lester Gray	34
4	Ellis Kinder	32
5	Glen Dacus, Walt Mestan	31
6	Tillman (Mike) Conovan	29
7	Bill Chambers, Dick Janasky	20
8	Joe Wesche	18
9	Charley Graves	17
10	Orlin Collier	15

Games

1	Jesse Webb	255
2	Lester Gray	84
3	Carl Gaiser	78
4	Tillman (Mike) Conovan	71
5	Glen Dacus	64
6	Charley Graves	53
7	Walt Mestan	52
8	Ellis Kinder	51
9	Leonard (Len) Hornsby	45
10	Bill Chambers	41

Losses

1	Jesse Webb	80
2	Tillman (Mike) Conovan	22
3	Lester Gray	21
4	Carl Gaiser	20
5	Glen Dacus	18
6	Leonard (Len) Hornsby	17
7	Bill Chambers	16
8	Dick Janasky, Ellis Kinder	15
9	Charley Graves	14
10	Walt Mestan	13

Complete Games

1	Jesse Webb	154
2	Carl Gaiser	56
3	Ellis Kinder	46
4	Glen Dacus	38
5	Lester Gray	37
6	Bill Chambers, Mike Conovan	34
7	Walt Mestan	30
8	Joe Wesche	25
9	Orlin Collier	21
10	Richard (Dick) Janasky	20

Winning Percentage (minimum 30 decisions)

1	Glen Dacus (22-8)	.733
2	Walt Mestan (31-13)	.705
3	Carl Gaiser (46-20)	.697
4	Ellis Kinder (32-15)	.681
5	Lester Gray (34-21)	.618
6	Jesse Webb (125-80)	.610
7	Joe Wesche (18-12)	.600
8	Dick Janasky (20-15)	.571
9	Mike Conovan (29-22)	.569
10	Bill Chambers (21-16)	.568

Innings Pitched

1	Jesse Webb	1,720
2	Carl Gaiser	602
3	Lester Gray	489
4	Glen Dacus	446
5	Ellis Kinder	432
6	Tillman (Mike) Conovan	414
7	Walt Mestan	375
8	Bill Chambers	314
9	Charley Graves	280
10	Richard (Dick) Janasky	268

Walks

1	Jesse Webb	643
2	Tillman (Mike) Conovan	250
3	Charley Graves	239
4	Bill Chambers	212
5	Walt Mestan	207
6	Carl Gaiser	175
7	Howard Ralph	163
8	Lester Gray	131
9	Ellis KInder	128
10	Glen Dacus	118

Strikeouts

1	Jesse Webb	1,532
2	Elli Kinder	486
3	Tillman (Mike) Conovan	452
4	Carl Gaiser	424
5	Charley Graves	311
6	Glen Dacus	300
7	Lester Gray	295
8	Walt Mestan	292
9	Bill Chambers	212
10	Joe Wesche	196

Earned Run Average (minimum 250 IP)

1	Ellis Kinder	2.58
2	Jesse Webb	2.69
3	Glen Dacus	2.74
4	Lester Gray	2.93
5	Bill Chambers	3.01
6	Walt Mestan	3.07
7	Richard (Dick) Janasky	3.22
8	Tillman (Mike) Conovan	3.59
9	Carl Gaiser	3.90
10	Charley Graves	5.82

*Excludes 1936 and 1942 seasons when earned runs were not tabulated in final statistics.

ELLIS KINDER

LESTER GRAY

Single-Season Batting Leaders 1935-1954

Games

Year	Player	Value
1935	Guy Jones	83
1936	Russell Newell	116
1937	C.C. Miller Jr.	115
1938	Louis (Lou) Perryman	128
1939	James (Jim) Kell	126
1940	Joe Polcha	123
1941	Melvin Merkel, Wallace Noon	126
1942	Ernie Ankrom, Lloyd Maloney, Ocky Walls	48
1950	Lee Valadez	120
1951	Harold (Hal) Seawright	118
1952	Robert (Bob) Grose	117
1953	Eddie Miller	112
1954	Harry Arterburn	26

Hits

Year	Player	Value
1935	Carl Sikes	106
1936	Ralph White	134
1937	C.C. (Cy) Miller Jr.	150
1938	Herbert (Dutch) Welch	154
1939	James (Jim) Kell	157
1940	Richard (Dick) Jones	156
1941	Wallace Noon	168
1942	Ernest (Ernie) Ankrom	65
1950	Maurice Partain	138
1951	Harold (Hal) Seawright	161
1952	Robert (Bob) Grose	110
1953	Vincent (Vince) Monaco	114
1954	Daniel (Danny) Meyers	33

At-Bats

Year	Player	Value
1935	Carl Sikes	337
1936	Russell Newell	484
1937	C.C. (Cy) Miller Jr.	452
1938	Richard (Dick) Jones	501
1939	James (Jim) Kell	540
1940	Al Cuozzo	473
1941	Wallace Noon	540
1942	Glen (Burper) Belcher	199
1950	Maurice Partain	476
1951	Harold (Hal) Seawright	478
1952	Robert (Bob) Grose	442
1953	Eddie Miller	441
1954	Harry Arterburn	107

Doubles

Year	Player	Value
1935	Anthony (Tony) Leidl	18
1936	Ralph White	23
1937	Herbert (Dutch) Welch	26
1938	Herbert (Dutch) Welch	37
1939	Vincent (Moon) Mullen	35
1940	Richard (Dick) Jones	35
1941	Ernest (Ernie) Ankrom	46
1942	Ocky Walls	11
1950	Glen (Gabby) Stewart	38
1951	Glen (Gabby) Stewart	33
1952	Dominic Italiano	18
1953	Eugene (Gene) Bennett	22
1954	Harry Arterburn	7

Runs

Year	Player	Value
1935	Carl Sikes	62
1936	Russell Newell	101
1937	C.C. (Cy) Miller Jr.	77
1938	C.C. (Cy) Miller Jr.	92
1939	Vincent (Moon) Mullen	100
1940	Joe Polcha	103
1941	Wallace Noon	121
1942	Lloyd Maloney	52

Runs (continued)

Year	Player	Value
1950	Maurice Partain	113
1951	Lee Valadez	107
1952	Robert (Bob) Grose	81
1953	Eddie Miller	81
	Charles (Chick) Re	81
1954	Mike Milinazzo	16

Triples

1935	James (Bull) Liddell	14
1936	Ralph White	11
1937	Herbert (Dutch) Welch	11
1938	Herbert (Dutch) Welch	11
1939	Lou Perryman	7
1940	Al Cuozzo	12
1941	Al Cuozzo	8
1942	Ernest (Ernie) Ankrom	4
1950	Robert (Bob) Samaras	6
1951	Glen (Gabby) Stewart	8
1952	Bob Grose, Lee Valadez	4
1953	Charles (Chick) Re	13
1954	Stewart Riles	2

Walks

1935	Not available	—
1936	Not available	—
1937	Russell Newell	69
1938	Vincent (Moon) Mullen	75
1939	Vincent (Moon) Mullen	97
1940	Joe Polcha	79
1941	Melvin (Mel) Merkel	91
1942	Lloyd Maloney	41
1950	Dominic Italiano	96
1951	Glen (Gabby) Stewart	92
1952	Robert (Bob) Grose	92
1953	Dominic Italiano	72
1954	Not available	—

Home Runs

1935	Anthony (Tony) Leidl	5
1936	Ralph White	10
1937	Duke Wells, Harold (Hal) Adair	4
1938	Vincent (Moon) Mullen	7
1939	Vincent (Moon) Mullen	8
1940	Gashouse Parker, Joe Polcha	27
1941	Melvin (Mel) Merkel	30
1942	Ernest (Ernie) Ankrom	7
1950	Harold (Hal) Seawright	9
1951	Harold (Hal) Seawright	16
1952	Dominic Italiano	8
1953	John Scercy	14
1954	Harry Arterburn, Mike Luciano, Danny Meyers, Mike Milinazzo	1

Strikeouts

1935	Not available	—
1936	Not available	—
1937	Russell Newell	38
1938	Louis (Lou) Perryman	44
1939	Vincent (Moon) Mullen	63
1940	Newt (Gashouse) Parker	128
1941	Melvin (Mel) Merkel	74
1942	Ray Riley	31
1950	Dominic Italiano	54
1951	Lee Valadez	47
1952	Robert (Bob) Grose	55
1953	John Scercy	97
1954	Not available	—

Runs Batted In

1935	Not available	—
1936	Ralph White	94
1937	C.C. (Cy) Miller Jr.	67
1938	Herbert (Dutch) Welch	69
1939	Vincent (Moon) Mullen	92
1940	Newt (Gashouse) Parker	109
1941	Melvin (Mel) Merkel	100
1942	Ernest (Ernie) Ankrom	54

Runs Batted In (continued)

1950	Glen (Gabby) Stewart	82
1951	Harold (Hal) Seawright	122
1952	Dominic Italiano	76
1953	Eugene (Gene) Bennett	83
1954	William (Bill) Hughes	17

Stolen Bases

1935	Carl Sikes	22
1936	Russell Newell	25
1937	C.C. (Cy) Miller Jr.	19
1938	Richard (Dick) Jones	23
1939	Richard (Dick) Jones	42
1940	Richard (Dick) Jones	51
1941	Andy Scarbola	27
1942	Ray Riley	17
1950	Maurice Partain	83
1951	Bearl Brooks	44
1952	Bearl Brooks, Robert Grose	14
1953	Edward (Eddie) Miller	21
1954	Charles Perkins	2

Batting Average (minimum 300 at-bats)

1935	Carl Sikes	.315
1936	Carl Sikes	.314
1937	C.C. (Cy) Miller Jr.	.332
1938	Herbert (Dutch) Welch	.319
1939	Richard (Dick) Jones	.313
1940	Richard (Dick) Jones	.338
1941	Al Cuozzo	.351
1942	Vincent Lepore	.349
1950	Maurice Partain	.299
1951	Harold (Hal) Seawright	.337
1952	Dominic Italiano	.274
1953	Vincent (Vince) Monaco	.316
1954	Daniel (Danny) Meyers	.359

1950 Generals Clyde Barger, Glen "Gabby" Stewart, Dominic Italiano, and Hayden Ray

Single-Season Pitching Leaders 1935-1954

Wins

1935	Joe Wesche	12
1936	Jesse Webb	18
1937	Jesse Webb	18
1938	Glen Dacus	22
1939	Ellis Kinder	17
1940	Ellis Kinder	21
1941	Carl Gaiser	26
1942	Leonard (Len) Hornsby	6
1950	Walt Mestan	16
1951	Bill Chambers	16
1952	Tillman (Mike) Conovan	20
1953	Ray D'Agrosa	14
1954	Richard Hardish	1

Games

1935	Buford Taylor	26
1936	Jesse Webb	35
1937	Jesse Webb	40
1938	Lester Gray	38
1939	Jesse Webb	41
1940	Jesse Webb	35
1941	Charley Graves, Jesse Webb	33
1942	Doyle Brady, Len Hornsby	16
1950	David Ross	30
1951	Bill Chambers	29
1952	Tillman (Mike) Conovan	47
1953	Howard Whitson	33
1954	James (Jim) Kluck	12

Losses

1935	Buford Taylor, Joe Wesche	8
1936	Jesse Webb	11
1937	Jesse Webb	14
1938	Jesse Webb	14
1939	Jesse Webb	13
1940	Jesse Webb	14
1941	Charley Graves, Len Hornsby	10
1942	Leonard (Len) Hornsby	7
1950	Tillman (Mike) Conovan	10
1951	Bill Chambers	11
1952	Howard Ralph	14
1953	Earl Gearhardt	13
1954	James (Jim) Kluck	6

Complete Games

1935	Joe Wesche	17
1936	Jesse Webb	28
1937	Jesse Webb	26
1938	Glen Dacus	23
1939	Jesse Webb	18
1940	Ellis Kinder	29
1941	Carl Gaiser	26
1942	Carl Gaiser	6
1950	Richard (Dick) Janasky	13
1951	Bill Chambers	24
1952	Tillman (Mike) Conovan	24
1953	Ray D'Agrosa, Earl Gearhardt, Howard Whitson	13
1954	James Kluck, Sonny Wilson	1

Winning Percentage (minimum 10 decisions)

1935	Jesse Webb (9-6)	.600
	Joe Wesche (12-8)	.600
1936	Jesse Webb (18-11)	.621
1937	Porter Witt (10-5)	.667
1938	Glen Dacus (22-8)	.733
1939	Lester Gray (16-11)	.593
1940	Ellis Kinder (21-9)	.700
1941	Carl Gaiser (26-5)	.839

Winning Percentage (continued)

1942	Doyle Brady (5-1)	.833
1950	Walt Mestan (16-5)	.762
1951	Walt Mestan (14-6)	.700
1952	Tillman (Mike) Conovan (20-12)	.625
1953	Ray D'Agrosa (14-7)	.667
1954	Richard Hardish (1-4)	.200

GENERALS BY THE NUMBERS

Innings Pitched

Year	Player	IP
1935	Joe Wesche	172
1936	Jesse Webb	248
1937	Jesse Webb	260
1938	Glen Dacus	249
1939	Jesse Webb	256
1940	Ellis Kinder	276
1941	Carl Gaiser	275
1942	Carl Gaiser	85
1950	Richard (Dick) Janasky	181
1951	Bill Chambers	220
1952	Tillman (Mike) Conovan	281
1953	Earl Gearhardt	184
1954	Richard Hardish	37.2

Strikeouts

Year	Player	K
1935	Joe Wesche	132
1936	Jesse Webb	227
1937	Jesse Webb	241
1938	Jesse Webb	225
1939	Ellis Kinder	200
1940	Ellis Kinder	307
1941	Jesse Webb	248
1942	Leonard (Len) Hornsby	55
1950	Richard (Dick) Janasky	130
1951	Bill Chambers	158
1952	Tillman (Mike) Conovan	345
1953	Ray D'Agrosa	158
1954	Vance Byrd, James Kluck	20

Walks

Year	Player	BB
1935	Jesse Webb	51
1936	Jesse Webb	96
1937	Jesse Webb	85
1938	Jesse Webb	105
1939	Jesse Webb	94
1940	Jesse Webb	113
1941	Charley Graves	162
1942	Leonard (Len) Hornsby	35
1950	Walt Mestan	88
1951	Bill Chambers	119
1952	Tillman (Mike) Conovan	224
1953	Ray D'Agrosa	95
1954	John Strunk	25

Earned Run Average

Year	Player	ERA
1935	Joe Wesche	2.87
1936	Not available	—
1937	Orlin Collier	2.73
1938	Glen Dacus	2.42
1939	Jesse Webb	3.09
1940	Ellis Kinder	2.38
1941	Ellis Kinder	2.88
1942	Carl Gaiser	3.12
1950	Richard (Dick) Janasky	3.38
1951	Bill Chambers	2.39
1952	Tillman (Mike) Conovan	3.46
1953	Howard Whitson	3.72
1954	Richard Hardish	7.26

GENERALS TEAM RECORDS 1935-1954

Year	Overall W-L	Pct.	First Half	Finish	Second Half	Finish	Managers
1935	(50-42)	.544	(21-23)	Fourth	(29-19)	First	Tony Leidl, Joe Wesche, Wilbur Bickham
1936	(61-56)	.521	(27-32)	Fifth	(34-24)	Third	Wilbur Bickham, Dutch Welch
1937	(63-58)	.521		Fifth*			Herbert (Dutch) Welch
1938	(74-54)	.578		Second			Herbert (Dutch) Welch
1939	(67-59)	.532		Fourth			Vincent (Moon) Mullen
1940	(67-57)	.540	(38-25)	First	(29-32)	Fifth	George (Mickey) O'Neil
1941	(84-43)	.661		First			George (Mickey) O'Neil
1942	(29-19)	.604		Third**			George (Mickey) O'Neil
1950	(68-52)	.567		Third			Glen (Gabby) Stewart
1951	(59-61)	.492		Fifth			Glen (Gabby) Stewart
1952	(48-71)	.403		Seventh			Vince Pankovits, Dominic Italiano, George (Mickey) O'Neil
1953	(58-62)	.483		Sixth			George (Mickey) O'Neil
1954	(1-41)***	.024		—			Lou Lukasiuk (Lucas)
Total	(679-633)	.518					

* Jackson lost a one-game playoff after finishing the regular season tied for fourth place with Mayfield

** Kitty League folded on June 18

*** Team owner Hiram Hopper returned the franchise to the Kitty League with a 1-26 record. The remaining games were forfeited to their scheduled opponents.

GENERALS POSTSEASON RECORDS 1935-1954

Year	W	L	Opponent		Manager	Notes
1935	—	—	—	—	Wilbur Bickham	Disqualified from second-half championship because of rule violation
1937	0	1	Mayfield Clothiers	—	Herbert (Dutch) Welch	One-game playoff for fourth place
1938	3	0	Lexington Bees	First	Herbert (Dutch) Welch	
1938	2	1	Hopkinsville Hoppers	Final	Herbert (Dutch) Welch	Hopkinsville canceled series due to cold weather and poor attendance
1940	3	4	Bowling Green Barons	First	George (Mickey) O'Neil	
1941	1	3	Mayfield Browns	First	George (Mickey) O'Neil	
1950	2	3	Fulton Railroaders	First	Glen (Gabby) Stewart	
Total	11	12				

Bibliography

Books and Publications

Finch, Robert L., L.H. Addington, and Ben M. Morgan, eds. *The Story of Minor League Baseball*. Columbus, OH: The National Association of Professional Baseball Leagues, 1952.
Halberstam, David. *Summer of '49*. New York: Avon Books, 1989
Honig, Donald. *Baseball Between the Lines: Baseball in the '40s and 50s as Told by the Men Who Played It*. New York: Coward, McCann, and Geoghegan, 1976.
Obojski, Robert. *Bush League: A History of Minor League Baseball*. New York: Mcmillan Publishing Company Inc., 1975.
Sullivan, Neil J. *The Minors: The Struggles and the Triumph of Baseball's Poor Relation from 1876 to the Present*. New York: St. Martin's Press, 1990.
West Tenn Diamond Jaxx. *1998 Official Media Guide*. Jackson, TN: Professional Sports and Entertainment Associates of Tennesssee, 1998.

Newspapers

Clarksville (TN) *Daily Leaf-Chronicle*
Hopkinsville *Kentucky New Era*
Jackson (TN) *Sun*
Memphis (TN) *Commercial Appeal*
Owensboro (KY) *Messenger-Inquirer*
Union City (TN) *Daily Messenger*

Interviews

Ernest Ankrom, Jim V. Bailey, Bearl Brooks, Mike Conovan, Carroll Drostie, John D. Graham, Charley Graves, Ray Haynes, Dominic Italiano, Richard (Dick) Janasky, Walt Mestan, Jim Murdaugh, Joe Wesche, Bernice (Mrs. Jesse Webb) Thompson, Howard Whitson

Other Resources

Files of *The Sporting News*, formerly located in St. Louis, Missouri
National Baseball Hall of Fame Library, Cooperstown New York
Baseball-Reference website (www.baseball-reference.com)

Index

Adair, Harold "Hal," 15, 19, 104
Addison, Leonard "Len," 58, 62, 63
Alabama State League, 11
All-Star Futures Game, 96
Allen, Kathleen, 86
Allen, Marlin, 86
American Association, 16, 93
American Basketball Association (ABA), 39
Ankrom, Ernest "Ernie," 37, 38, 41, 43, 46, 47, 48, 50, 51, 52, 53, 98, 99, 102, 103, 104
Anniston, AL, 53
Antonelli, Johnny, 20
Arkansas A & M College, 19
Arterburn, Harry, 85, 87, 90, 103, 104
Atlanta Braves, 12
Atkins, AR, 23
AuBuchon, Fred, 67, 74
AuBuchon, Leon, 74

Babe Ruth League (Jackson, TN), 92
Baker, Fred, 3, 18, 35, 37, 45
Bailey, Raymond E. "Tobe" Jr., 36, 66
Bailey, Jim V., 74, 80, 82, 97
Baltimore Orioles, 95
Baltimore, MD, 39
Barger, Clyde, 55, 57, 60, 62, 63, 65, 69, 96, 100, 105
Barrett, Gordon, 14
Bassett, Dr. Frank H., 2, 6, 14
Beggs, Ellis, 12
Belcher, Glen "Burper," 50, 51, 52, 53, 103
Bell, Bob Jr., 25
Bemis Square Shopping Center, 3
Bemis, TN, 10
Bennett, Eugene "Gene," 78, 82, 83, 103, 104
Bergel, Sam, 39
Berra, Yogi, 36, 73
Bickham, Wilbur, 1, 4, 5, 7, 9, 10, 11
Bierman, Howard, 72

Black, Paul, 27
Bloomington, IL, 44
Boom (proposed team name), 94
Boston Bees, 23
Boston Braves, 35, 52, 57, 73
Boston Red Sox, 11, 36, 39
Bowling Green, KY, 28, 67, 90
Bowling Green (KY) Barons, 11, 31, 32, 33, 37, 41, 42, 44, 45, 47, 49, 52, 53
Brady, Doyle, 50, 51, 52, 106
Bragan, Jimmy, 93
Brashers Clothing Store (Jackson, TN), 36
Bray, Julian, 1, 5, 7, 8, 15
Brewer, Robert, 72
Brooklyn Dodgers, 8, 23, 66, 79
Brooklyn Robins, 35
Brooklyn, NY, 8, 39
Brooks, Bearl, 55, 58, 61, 63, 65, 69, 70, 72, 73, 99, 100, 105
Bryja, Walt, 66
Burham Field (Dyersburg, TN), 74
Burgess, Lloyd, 80
Burlington, IA, 79
Byrd, Vance, 85, 87, 88, 90, 107

Cairo, IL, 2, 57, 61, 66
Cairo (IL) Dodgers, 57, 58, 64, 66, 71
California Angels, 12
Callahan, Perry H., 44
Callahan, Walter, 39
Canadian-American League, 53, 54
Cape Girardeau, MO, 8
Carraway, Andrew, 95, 96
Carswell, James, 87, 89
Carter, Aubrey, 1
Catricala, Vinnie, 95, 96
Central City, KY, 90
Central City (KY) Reds, 90, 91

Chambers, Bill, 55, 59, 60, 61, 63, 65, 66, 67, 68, 69, 101, 102, 106, 107
Charlotte (NC) Knights, 93
Chattanooga (TN) Lookouts, 95
Chicago, IL, 66
Chicago Cubs, 23, 26, 88, 90, 95
Chicago White Sox, 12, 36, 57, 79
Chivers, Arthur "Art," 65
Christmasville Road (Jackson, TN), 93
Cincinnati, OH, 52
Cincinnati Reds, 8, 16, 79, 87
Clark, Chuck, 93, 94
Clarksville, TN, 86, 90
Clarksville (TN) Colts, 56
Cleveland Indians, 16, 23
Clonts, Ray, 14
Coca-Cola Bottling Works (Jackson, TN), 8
Collier, Orlin, 15, 16, 17, 19, 20, 21, 76, 101, 107
Colorado Rockies, 93
Commerce, GA, 19
Conovan, Tillman "Mike," 55, 58, 60, 72, 73, 74, 75, 76, 96, 97, 101, 102, 106, 107
Corinth, MS, 8
Corrillo, Juan, 80
Cotton States League, 56, 58, 73
Crofton, KY, 88
Cummings, Clarence "Polly," 20
Cuozzo, Alfonse "Al," 34, 37, 38, 39, 40, 41, 43, 44, 46, 47, 48, 99, 100, 103, 104, 105

D'Agrosa, Ray, 78, 79, 80, 81, 82, 83, 106, 107
Dacus, Glen, 22, 23, 24, 26, 27, 28, 31, 32, 101, 102, 106, 107
Daidone, Joe, 80
Danville, IL, 11
Deary, Barney, 70
Death Valley (Jackson, TN), 79, 92
Debnar, Paul, 20
Del Rio, Roy, 65, 66
DeMasi, Joe, 62
Des Ormeaux, Jane, 94, 95
Detroit, MI, 29
Detroit Tigers, 12, 13, 17, 44, 52, 87
Dexter, MO, 12

Diamond Jacks (proposed team name), 94
Diamond Jaxx (see West Tenn Diamond Jaxx)
Dillon, Charles, 85, 87
Dixon, Paul, 34
Dodd, Fayette, 23, 25, 29
Dorris, Joe, 18
Dover, TN, 24
Drake, Ben, 27, 28, 31, 32
Drostie, Carroll, 78, 79, 80, 81, 82, 96, 97
Drye, Claude, 49
Duhem, Joseph, 70
Durdin, Matt, 1, 2
Dyersburg, TN, 11, 20, 52, 73, 74, 86, 90

Eastham, Lonnie, 72, 79, 80
Edmondton Trappers, 93
Elam, Wade, 26
Elder, Jerry, 78, 82, 83
Evans, Robert "Bob," 55, 58, 59, 60
Exum, Fred, 38

Fairfield Park (Fulton, KY), 69, 76, 82
Farmer, Charles, 93, 94
Farnsworth, Kyle, 95
Fielkow, Arnie, 94
Florence, AL, 9
Florida Marlins, 93
Ford Motor V-8 club (Memphis semi-pro team), 9
Forked Deer River, 92
Forrest, Billy Joe, 67
Foust, A.B., 23, 38
Francis, Will Ed, 28
Frazier, Roy, 14
Freed-Hardeman College (Henderson, TN), 9, 10
Freed-Hardeman University (Henderson, TN), 11
Freedman, Irvin, 56
Friskel, Robert, 72
Fulton (KY) Chicks, 54, 58
Fulton (KY) Eagles, 10, 12, 13, 14, 16, 19, 23, 24, 26, 32, 33
Fulton (KY) Lookouts, 73, 75, 76, 77, 79, 81, 82, 83, 84, 88, 89, 91
Fulton (KY) Railroaders, 11, 57, 61, 62, 63, 64, 66, 67, 71, 97

INDEX

Fulton (KY) Tigers, 40, 42, 44, 49, 52, 53
Fulton, KY, 8, 69

Gaiser, Carl, 27, 28, 32, 34, 37, 39, 40, 42, 43, 44, 45, 46, 47, 48, 50, 53, 101, 102, 106, 107
Garagiola, Joe, 36, 73
Garden Plaza Hotel (Jackson, TN), 97
Gasell, John, 44
Gates, Jimmy, 40
Gearhardt, Earl, 78, 79, 82, 96, 97, 106, 107
Gibbs, Bert, 70
Gilland, Hartle G., 3, 6, 30, 35, 37, 39, 41, 42, 44, 48, 53
Gilland, Shaler "Preacher," 3, 5, 20, 35, 36, 37, 42, 44
Gillheeney, James, 96
Gilliam, Richard, 78
Giordano, Tom, 87
Glenn, Sam, 24
Golden, Paul, 25
Goodman, Billy, 36
Goodwin, James, 29, 32, 45, 46, 51
Gordon, Earl, 80
Graham, John D., 29, 48, 86, 88, 89, 92
Graves, Charley, 34, 37, 38, 39, 43, 44, 46, 47, 101, 102, 106, 107
Gray, Lester, 13, 22, 24, 26, 27, 28, 30, 31, 101, 102, 106
Greenville, MS, 58
Griffin, Ewing, 44
Griffith, Earl "Country," 34, 37, 40
Grissom, Ray, 51
Grose, Robert "Bob," 72, 103, 104, 105
Grossman, Harley, 63
Grube, Jarrett, 95

Haas, Elmer "Lefty," 23, 26, 41
Hahn, Earl, 1, 5, 10, 14
Hamlin, Jimmy, 59, 73, 92
Hannephin, James Edgar "Ed," 25, 29
Hardish, Richard, 85, 87, 90, 106, 107
Hayden, Stanley, 15
Hayes, Allen "Shorty," 9
Haynes, Ray, 43, 47
Hazard, KY, 66

Hazelton, Don, 61
Heery International, 94
Helena, AR, 73
Helvey, Bob, 16
Henderson, KY, 90
Henderson, Paul, 48, 49
Henry, Fred, 65, 70
Herron, Dr. Henry, 86
Hersh, David, 94
Hiram's Restaurant (Jackson, TN), 74, 86
Hodge, Elbert, 7
Hopkinsville, KY, 31, 88
Hopkinsville (KY) Hoppers, 2, 4, 5, 6, 9, 10, 11, 12, 14, 16, 17, 20, 23, 24, 25, 26, 30, 32, 33, 42, 44, 46, 47, 48, 49, 52, 53, 57, 59, 61, 64, 68, 70, 71, 74, 75, 76, 77, 79, 83, 84,
Hopper, Hiram, 74, 76, 80, 81, 86, 88, 89, 90, 92, 93
Hopper, Jeff, 87
Hopper, Rachel, 74
Hornsby, Leonard "Len," 43, 47, 50, 51, 52, 53, 101, 106, 107
Hornsby, Mickey, 48
Hot Springs, AR, 56
House of David team, 16, 23
Houston, TX, 12
Howard, Ben F., 28, 37
Howe, David, 22, 24
Hub City Taxi Company, 74
Hubbard, Cecil, 59, 63
Huff, Bob, 87
Hughes, Bill, 85, 87, 104
Hughes, Frank, 16
Humboldt (TN) Shoemakers, 28
Huntingdon, WV, 66
Husick, John 80
Huss, Roland, 80
Hutchinson, KS, 45
Hutson, Cecil, 16, 25, 26

Illinois Central Railroad, 29
International League, 21
Irwin, Scott, 65

Italiano, Dominic, 55, 57, 58, 59, 61, 63, 68, 72, 73, 74, 75, 76, 78, 79, 80, 82, 96, 99, 100, 103, 104, 105

Jackson Baseball Association, Inc., 56, 66, 67, 68, 73, 74, 92
Jackson (TN) City Council, 93, 94
Jackson Generals Boosters, 37, 38
Jackson-Madison County (TN) Sports Hall of Fame, 11, 18
Jackson, MS, 44, 73
Jackson (TN) High School, 68
Jackson (TN) High School band, 44
Jackson (TN) Independents, 29
Jackson (TN) Midwests (semi-pro club), 2, 3, 11, 19
Jackson Sun, 25, 45, 46, 86, 88, 92, 94
Jackson Transportation Company, 37, 74
Jacksonville, FL, 96
Jamestown, NY, 86
Janasky, Richard "Dick," 55, 57, 58, 59, 60, 63, 65, 68, 69, 101, 102, 106, 107
Janse, John, 51
Jaynes, J.T., 68
Jernigan, Dean, 94
Johnson, Judge Frank L., 20
Johnson, Ira, 86
Jones, Guy, 1, 6, 103
Jones, Joe, 85
Jones, Richard "Dick," 22, 24, 26, 27, 31, 32, 34, 37, 39, 41, 44, 46, 99, 100, 103, 105
Junior Chamber of Commerce (Jackson, TN), 67, 86, 92
Junior Generals, 66
Justice, Bill, 12

Kansas City Monarch, 75
Kasparek, Kenn, 95
Kell, James "Jim," 27, 28, 31, 103
Keller, Lee, 14
Kimble, Dick, 49
Kinder, Ellis, 3, 23, 27, 28, 30, 31, 32, 34, 36, 37, 38, 39, 40, 41, 43, 44, 46, 47, 49, 76, 101, 102, 106, 107
Kirik, Emil, 55, 59, 63, 96

Kitty League All-Star Game, 12, 20, 31, 39, 40, 46, 59, 60, 61, 69, 75, 76, 81
Klein, Lou, 36
Kluck, James "Jim," 65, 67, 68, 85, 87, 89, 106, 107
Knickerbocker, Austin, 83
Knickmeyer, Walter, 11
Knight, John, 86
Kolomay, Richard "Dick," 80
Kovaleski, Stan, 87
Krawezak, Joeph, 61
Kreiger, Ed, 58
Kubek, Tony, 88
Kvedar, Tony, 46

LaFromboise, Bobby, 95
LaGrange, GA, 45
Lakeview Cafe, 3
Lakeview Park (Jackson, TN), 3, 8, 10, 13, 19, 20, 23, 25, 28, 29, 30, 32, 35, 37, 38, 41, 42, 44, 46, 47, 48, 52, 53
Lakeview Tourist Camp, 3
Lambert, Odell "Dolly," 7, 8, 11, 23
Lambuth College (Jackson, TN), 17, 28
Landis, Kenesaw Mountain, 41
Latshaw, Bob, 90
Leaksville, NC, 45
Leidl, Anthony, 1, 2, 4, 6, 103, 104
Lepore, Vincent, 105
Liddell, James "Bull," 1, 4, 5, 6, 7, 8, 9, 11, 12, 99, 104
Lisenbee, Harold M. "Hod," 56
Livingston, Sam, 12
Lepore, Vincent, 50, 105
Lexington (TN) Bees, 23, 25, 26,
Lexington (TN) Giants, 2, 4, 6, 8, 10, 13, 14, 16, 17, 19
Long, John B., 12
Longview, TX, 28
Loudon, TN, 82
Lovelady, Jimmy, 1
Lucas, Lou (Lulasiuk), 85, 86, 87, 88, 89, 90
Luciano, Mike, 85, 104
Lyter, William, 15

INDEX

McCarthy, Joe, 36
McCoy, Harold, 1, 21
McDevitt, Leland, 11
McGhay, Gerald, 89
McGhee, Casey, 95
McGraw, John, 35
McKechnie, Bill. Jr., 79, 81
McLeod, George, 82
McMillan, Chuck, 87

Mad Jacks (proposed team name), 94
Madisonville, KY, 88
Madisonville (KY) Miners, 57, 59, 61, 62, 64, 67, 69, 70, 71, 77, 79, 80, 81, 83, 84, 88, 89, 90, 91
Majors, Jim, 87
Maloney, Lloyd, 43, 44, 46, 47, 50, 51, 52, 53, 103, 104
Marion, KY, 31
Marmol, Carlos, 95
Martin, Babe, 36
Martin, Charles, 37, 41
Martin, Clyde, 7, 11, 12, 15, 16, 19, 24, 27
Martin, John D., 2
Martindale, Leo, 57, 58, 73
Martinez, Frank, 87
Mason, R.W. "Bubba," 2, 5
May, Joe, 72, 73
Mayfield (KY) Browns, 29, 31, 32, 33, 38, 40, 42, 48, 49, 51, 54
Mayfield (KY) Clothiers, 8, 9, 13, 14, 16, 20, 21, 23, 25, 26, 57, 58, 59, 61, 62, 63, 64, 67, 69, 70, 71, 73, 76, 77, 83, 84, 91
Medina, TN, 12, 20, 37, 54
Medon, TN, 76
Meeks, Mrs. George, 96
Memphis Chicks, 4, 8, 10, 11, 18, 36, 52, 93, 94
Memphis Redbirds, 94
Memphis, TN, 10, 97
Men's Night, 30
Merkel, Melvin "Mel," 22, 23, 24, 25, 26, 34, 37, 39, 40, 41, 42, 43, 45, 46, 47, 48, 69, 99, 100, 103, 104
Mestan, Walt, 55, 58, 59, 60, 61, 62, 63, 65, 66, 67, 68, 69, 70, 95, 96, 97, 101, 102, 106, 107

Meyers, Daniel, 85, 87, 103, 105
Milinazzo, Mike, 85, 87, 88, 90, 103, 104
Miller, C.C. "Cy," Jr., 15, 16, 17, 19, 20, 22, 24, 99, 100, 103, 104, 105
Miller, Eddie, 78, 80, 82, 103, 105
Miller Park (Owensboro, KY), 17
Mills, Ivan "Hambone," 78, 79, 80, 82
Mills, Thomas Lee, 87
Milan, TN, 57, 69, 90
Milwaukee Brewers, 16
Minor, Ray, 48
Miss Jackson General Beauty Contest, 68
Mississippi-Ohio Valley League, 56
Mississippi State College, 5
Molina, Jose, 95
Monaco, Vince, 78, 82, 103, 105
Monette, AR, 58
Morehouse, Robert, 87
Morgan, William "Buster," 22, 24, 25, 26, 27, 31, 100
Morristown, TN, 12, 17
Mountain States League, 73
Mucci, Peter R., 86, 88
Mueller, John, 51
Mullen, Vincent "Moon," 18, 22, 24, 25, 27, 28, 30, 31, 32, 35, 40, 44, 99, 100, 103, 104
Municipal Park (Jackson, TN), 56, 57, 59, 60, 63, 67, 69, 71, 74, 75, 76, 79, 80, 81, 82, 83, 86, 87, 88, 89, 90, 92
Murdaugh, James "Jim," 7, 10, 15
Murphy, Fred, 20
Murray, Tom, 86

Nashville, TN, 58
Nashville (TN) *Banner*, 89
Nashville Vols, 8, 16, 57
National Association of Professional Baseball Leagues, 5, 74
Negro American League, 75
Nehf, Art, 35
New Orleans Pelicans, 10
New York Giants, 35, 52, 56
New York Yankees, 12, 36, 38, 44, 46, 73, 79, 88
Newell, Russell Jr., 7, 8, 10, 11, 14, 15, 16, 99, 100, 103, 104, 105

Newkirk, Bill, 78, 82
Nichols, Gene, 5
Nicklous, Mike, 93
Noon, Wallace "Wally," 43, 44, 46, 47, 48, 103
Northern League, 87

O'Connell, Eddie, 20
O'Neil, George Mickey, 3, 34, 35, 37, 38, 39, 40, 41, 43, 44, 45, 46, 47, 48, 49, 51, 53, 54, 76, 79, 80, 82, 83, 84
O'Rourke, Steve, 38
O'Toole, Patsy, 29

Oakland Athletics, 12
Ogden, UT, 79
Oman, Eric, 82
Orlando, Angie, 67
Owens, Johnny, 15, 21
Owensboro, KY, 8, 12, 16, 17
Owensboro (KY) Pirates, 14
Owensboro (KY) Oilers, 16, 20, 23, 25, 26, 28, 29, 31, 33, 38, 40, 41, 42, 47, 49, 52, 53, 57, 58, 59, 61, 62, 64, 67, 68, 70, 71, 76, 77, 79, 83, 84, 88, 91

Pace, John G., 20
Pacific Coast League, 93
Paducah, KY, 12, 30, 66, 97
Paducah (KY) Chiefs, 66, 70, 71, 76, 77, 79, 81, 83, 84, 91
Paducah (KY) Indians, 8, 12, 14, 16, 19, 25, 26, 33, 38, 40, 42, 49, 51, 88, 90
Paducah (KY) Red Birds, 2, 4
Paige, Satchel, 75
Pankovits, Jim, 95
Pankovits, Vince, 73, 95
Parham, Chester, 86
Paris, TN, 90
Paris (TN) Parisians, 11
Parker, Newt "Gashouse," 34, 35, 37, 38, 39, 40, 42, 43, 44, 45, 46, 100, 104
Partain, Maurice "Maury," 55, 58, 59, 61, 62, 65, 69, 99, 100, 103, 105
Patterson, Corey, 95
Pavlige, Bill, 28, 31

Paxton, James, 96
Peace, Shelby, 51, 61, 74, 81, 88, 90
Pearl Harbor, 51
Pennington Gap, WV, 73
Perkins, Charles, 85, 87, 105
Perryman, Louis "Lou," 22, 24, 27, 28, 31, 32, 98, 99, 104
Pfautz, John, 83
Philadelphia Athletics, 52, 79
Philadelphia Phillies, 56
Piedmont League, 53, 69
Pierson, Victor, 65, 70, 72, 73
Pioneer League, 79
Pittsburgh Pirates, 45, 57
Pleasantville, NJ, 79
Pringles Park (Jackson, TN), 94, 95, 96
Prior, Mark, ix, 95
Proctor and Gamble Company, 95
Polcha, Joe, 34, 37, 38, 39, 40, 41, 42, 44, 46, 99, 100, 103, 104
Polo Grounds, 56
PONY League, 86
Portageville (MO) Pirates, 2, 4, 5, 6, 8, 10, 11, 12
Portsmouth (VA) Cubs, 69
Pratt, Ed, 87
Protho, Doc, 18
Pruett, Doyle, 58, 62

Quillen, Bo "Mutt," 11

Ralph, Howard, 69, 72, 73, 76, 102, 106
Ramirez, Erasmo, 95
Raschi, Vic, 36
Ray, Hayden, 55, 58, 105
Re, Charles "Chick," 78, 81, 82, 96, 97, 103, 104
Reasner, Jack, 8, 10
Reed, Billy, 58
Reeder, Charles, 50
Reese, Eddie, 19
Reist, Mel, 37, 41, 42, 43, 45, 47, 52
Resinger, Grover, 1, 6, 7, 8, 10, 12, 15, 20, 99, 100, 105
Rice, Russell, 56, 61, 74
Richards, Bobby, 12
Richmond (VA) Blues, 53

INDEX

Riles, Stewart, 85, 87, 104
Riley, Ray, 50, 51, 104, 105
Ritter, Wallace, 25, 26
Robinson, Aaron, 56, 68
Robinson, Ann, 2
Robinson, Everett, 84
Roosevelt, Franklin D., 51
Ross, David, 58, 60, 71, 106
Ross, Edgar, 34
Roth, Ritchie, 79, 80, 82
Rowley, Larry, 80
Royal Rooters, 29

Samaras, Robert "Bob," 55, 59, 63, 104
Santa, Ed, 69
Savro, Pat, 57
Scarbola, Andy, 43, 45, 46, 47, 100, 105
Scercy, John, 78, 82, 83, 96, 97, 100, 104
Schmitz, Johnny, 26
Schumacher, Howard, 29
Scolpini, Bucky, 51
Scott, Chauncey, 24
Scottsville, AR, 36
Seager, Kyle, 95
Seattle Mariners, 95
Seawright, Harold "Hal," 55, 58, 59, 61, 62, 63, 65, 69, 70, 99, 100, 103, 104, 105
Shaffer, Jake, 95
Shaughnessy, Frank, 21
Sheanshang, Tony, 51
Sheridan, Tom, 80, 87
Sherman, Bob, 82
Shirley, Elmer "Mule," 20
Shreveport, LA, 10
Sikes, Carl, 1, 4, 6, 7, 12, 13, 99, 103, 105
Sikes, Watts, 5
Silvers, Charlie, 15
Simmons, Bill, 87
Simpson, Harold, 56
Sisler, Dick, 36
Sly, Bud, 40
Smith, George, 36
Smith, Ralph, 50, 51, 52
Slaughter, Enos, 12

Sosa, Sammy, ix, 95
Southard, Norman, 45, 49
Southeastern League, 44, 53
Southern Association, 10, 16, 57
Southern League, 93, 94, 95
Southern League All-Star Game, ix, 95
Speas, Chris, 83
Starkville, MS, 4
St. Louis Browns, 13, 14, 23, 36, 73
St. Louis Cardinals, 8, 14, 23, 35, 36, 52, 73, 79, 86, 92
St. Louis, MO, 12, 28, 31, 35, 57, 73
St. Louis Post-Dispatch, 89, 92
Stein, Steve, 86
Stengel, Casey, 35
Stevens, Don, 58, 62
Stevens Point, WI, 67
Stewart, Glen "Gabby," 55, 56, 58, 59, 61, 63, 65, 69, 70, 73, 97, 99, 100, 103, 104, 105
Stewart, Richard "Dick," 22, 23
Stockham American Legion team (St. Louis, MO), 73
Storie, Burl, 69
Strunk, Jack, 85, 88, 107
Stubblefield, Mickey, 75
Superior (WI) Blues, 87
Surgaliski, John, 1, 4, 5, 6
Suther, John Henry, 5
Swank, John, 13
Sweatt, Bill, 54
Swisher, Robert, 61
Sventko, Andy, 62

Tate, Benny, 29
Tate, Charles, 62
Taylor, Buford, 1, 2, 9, 106
Taylor, Harve, 16
Tennessee Smokies, 95
Texas League, 45
The Hill (St. Louis, MO), 73
The Pit Cafe and Steak House (Bemis, TN), 53
The Sporting News, 89
Thomas, Dick, 70
Thomas, Golden, 22

Thomas, Joseph, 72
Three-I League, 11, 79
Three Rivers club, 53
Tim McCarver Stadium (Memphis, TN), 94
Toledo Mud Hens, 35
Topp, Edd, 86
Trautman, George, 74
Trembley, Dave, 95
Troy, NY, 39
Tullahoma, TN, 56
Tulsa, OK, 45
Turlington, Charles, 32
Turner Field (Union City, TN), 11

University of Alabama, 5
University of Kentucky, 59
Union City (TN) Dodgers, 79, 80, 81, 84, 87, 91
Union City (TN) Greyhounds, 2, 5, 6, 8, 9, 11, 12, 13, 14, 16, 17, 18, 19, 20, 21, 23, 25, 33, 38, 42, 44, 48, 49, 52, 53, 54, 57, 59, 61, 64, 66, 67, 70, 71, 73, 75, 76, 77
Union University (Jackson, TN), 79
Urbon, Eddie, 29, 40

Valadez, Lee, 55, 58, 61, 65, 72, 73, 75, 76, 99, 100, 103, 104
Valenzano, Vito, 72
Valine, George, 20
Vander Meer, Johnny, 79
Vanderbilt Law School, 17
Vangilder, Elam, 13
Veazey, Norman, 15
Vinson, Casie, 47

Wahl, Sam, 56
Waldrop, Ned, 63, 82, 97
Walker, Fred, 21, 24, 27, 28, 31
Walker, James, 40
Walkup, Roy, 55, 58, 60, 62
Walling, Cliff, 72, 74, 75
Walls, Ocky, 50, 51, 103
Ware, Lee, 23
Washington Senators, 35, 56, 79

Webb, Jesse, 1, 2, 3, 5, 7, 9, 12, 13, 14, 15, 16, 17, 18, 20, 22, 23, 24, 25, 27, 28, 30, 31, 32, 34, 37, 38, 39, 40, 43, 44, 46, 47, 48, 50, 51, 52, 54, 99, 101, 102, 106, 107
Webb, John D., 6
Wehman, Richard "Dick," 78, 82, 83
Weiser, Mel, 67, 68
Welch, Herbert "Dutch," 3, 7, 11, 15, 16, 19, 20, 21, 22, 24, 99, 100, 103, 104, 105
Wells, Duke, 15, 17, 19, 20, 21, 104
Wenning, Elmer, 9, 14, 23, 24, 26
Wesche, Joe, 1, 2, 4, 6, 7, 9, 101, 102, 106, 107
West Tenn Diamond Jaxx (Jackson, TN), 94, 95
West Tennessee State Fairgrounds (Jackson, TN), 92, 93
Western Association, 45
White, Bud, 34
White, Ralph L., 7, 8, 9, 12, 19, 23, 31, 100, 104
Whitson, Howard, 78, 79, 80, 81, 82, 83, 106, 107
Wilburn, Chet "Wimpy," 44
Williams, Archie, 15, 19, 24, 26
Williams, Charlie, 56
Williams, Harry, 37, 41
Williams, Tom "Cy," 1, 4
Wilson, Lindsey, 14
Wilson, Sonny, 87, 106
Wise, Hugh, 20, 41
Witt, Porter, 15, 16, 17, 24, 106
Womack, E.L., 86
Wright, Ed, 23, 50, 52
WTJS Radio (Jackson, TN), 8
Wylam, AL, 4

YMCA Building (Jackson, TN), 96

Zambrano, Carlos, 95
Zawacki, John, 87

About the Author

Kevin D. McCann is a Jackson, Tennessee native and graduated with a Bachelor of Science Degree from Union University. He has researched the colorful history of the Jackson Generals and the Kitty League for 15 years. Mr. McCann is the author of *Jackson Diamonds: Professional Baseball in Jackson, Tennessee* and co-author of *The Kitty League*, part of Arcadia Publishing's Images of Baseball series. He lives with his wife Cindy and children Braden and Brianna in Dickson, Tennessee.

www.ingramcontent.com/pod-product-compliance
Lightning Source LLC
Chambersburg PA
CBHW080545090426
42734CB00016B/3202